湖北省博物馆
HUBEI PROVINCIAL MUSEUM

郧县人

长江中游的远古人类

Yunxian Man

Prehistoric People in the Middle Reaches of the Yangtze

■ 湖北省博物馆 编
Hubei Provincial Museum

文物出版社
Cultural Relics Press

目 录 CONTENTS

序

湖北历史悠久，文化遗存丰富。截至目前，湖北境内已普查出不可移动文物点1.5万余处，其中全国重点文物保护单位90处，省级文物保护单位457处，武当山古建筑群、钟祥明显陵先后被列入世界文化遗产名录。无论是文物点的总量，还是文物单位的保护级别，湖北都位居全国前列。

中华人民共和国成立后的考古工作，完全改写了湖北的历史，证实这里同样是中华文明的生长点。两个完整的、距今100万年的直立人——"郧县人"头骨的发现，证明这里也是探索人类起源最重要的地区之一；距今5000年的"屈家岭文化"以发达的稻作农业，功能齐全的史前城址，昭示这里同样是文明起源的发源地；商代的"盘龙城"、两周时期的铜绿山古矿冶遗址和被誉为"地下乐宫"的曾侯乙墓的发现，说明这里的青铜文明同样绚丽多彩；江陵纪南城、望山楚墓、马山楚墓，荆门包山楚墓、郭店楚墓，枣阳九连墩楚墓等重要考古发现，印证楚文化曾在湖北地区达到鼎盛时期；大量秦汉至唐宋遗存的发现，以及明代楚昭王、郢靖王和梁庄王等一批明代藩王墓的发掘，丰富了地方文化历史的研究资料。

负责全省文物保护、收藏、展示的湖北省博物馆，于1953年3月成立筹备处；1959年春迁至今址东湖风景区；1963年1月正式更名为湖北省博物馆，3000平方米的陈列楼建成并对外开放；1999年1月，建筑面积5717平方米的编钟馆建成开放；2005年12月，楚文化馆建成开放；2007年9月，新馆综合陈列馆建成开放。至此，湖北省博物馆总占地面积达81909平方米，建筑面积49611平方米，展厅面积13427平方米，馆藏文物14万余件（套），其中一级文物千余件（套），位居全国省级博物馆前列。

借新馆综合陈列馆开放之机，我们一改过去通史陈列的方式，根据馆藏文物特点，新推出了十一个专题陈列。《郧县人——长江中游的远古人类》以镇馆之宝"郧县人"的发现为主线，扩展至湖北境内旧石器时代遗存的发现，辅以世界范围内早期人类起源的资料，试图使观众对早期人类的生活有个概略的了解；《屈家岭——长江中游的史前文化》则上推至距今8000多年前的城背溪文化，下连到距今4000年前的石家河文化，力图全方位地揭示长江中游地区新石器时代农业的发生、人类的定居生活以及文明的发生过程；《盘

龙城——长江中游的青铜文明》展示的是商代"南土"今黄陂盘龙城城址的考古发现，
证实由于大冶铜绿山铜矿资源系统的存在，促使商文化南下，客观上促进了长江中游的
文明进程；《曾侯乙墓》是我馆的精品陈列，这次展览在原有的基础上，展示面积有所
扩大，展品也有所增加，较为全面地反映了曾侯乙时代的礼乐文化；《九连墩纪事》重
点讲述的是九连墩的考古发掘过程和楚国高级贵族墓的墓葬文化；《秦汉漆器艺术》将
我馆所藏最具特色的秦汉漆器集中展示，对漆器的制作工艺和艺术特点作了重点阐释；
《书写历史——战国秦汉简牍》是举办同类展览的一个新的尝试，即以湖北出土的战国
秦汉简牍和书写工具实物为主，上溯至原始社会的刻划符号和陶文，辅以世界各地的书
写历史背景，使观众对书写的历史有个较全面的了解；《土与火的艺术——古代瓷器专
题展》以青瓷、青花瓷、官窑瓷器为重点，展示了馆藏瓷器的精品；《梁庄王墓——郑
和时代的瑰宝》展示的是明代梁庄王墓的出土遗物；《明清书画——湖北省博物馆藏书
画展》从馆藏书画中选取了明清时期较有代表性的绘画、书法流派人物的作品予以介
绍；《荆楚百年英杰》展示了近代以来，对中国近现代历史、科学文化和经济建设有过
重要影响和做出突出贡献的湖北籍或在湖北长期工作过的革命家、历史人物、文化俊杰
和科教精英的简要生平事迹，旨在让人们永远记住他们。这些展览力图通过不同的截
面，展示湖北历史和文化的闪光点，通过文物来勾画湖北历史发展进程的粗略线条，让
观众在此领略我们祖先的聪明才智，也使我馆成为人们心灵对话、交流的场所，成为人
们追求精神生活不可或缺的精神家园。

　　为配合展览，我们推出了这套"长江中游文明之旅"丛书，每本书都还约请有关专家
撰写文章，或概要介绍文化背景，或集中阐述文化内涵。每本书都以文物图片为主，辅以
简单的说明。总的目的是为读者能够方便和深入地了解湖北的地方历史和文化，并保留一
份记忆。

湖 北 省 博 物 馆 馆 长
湖北省文物考古研究所所长
湖北省文物保护中心主任

Preface

长江中游文明之旅

A Journey to Mid-Yangtze River Civilization

Hubei, which has a long history, abounds in cultural heritages. Up to now, more than 15,000 immoveable sites have been registered, including 90 major historic sites under national protection and 457 under provincial protection. The ancient architectural complex at Wudangshan and Xian Mausoleum of the Ming Dynasty in Zhongxiang have been inscribed into World Heritage List. The province ranks high in the country in both the number and the protection grades of sites.

Since the founding of the PRC, archaeological research has totally changed the history of Hubei, proving that it was also one of the origins of the Chinese civilization. The discovery of two integral crania of Yunxian Man, a *Homo erectus* species dating from one million years ago, shows that Hubei is one of the most important regions for exploring the origin of human being. Qujialing Culture, which dates from 5,000 years ago, with well-developed rice-growing agriculture and functionally complete prehistoric sites, indicates that the region was a cradle of civilization. Panlongcheng of the Shang Dynasty, the mining and smelting site at Tonglüshan of the Zhou Dynasty, and the tomb of Marquis Yi of Zeng, which is called 'underground musical palace', reflect a brilliant bronze civilization. Jinancheng at Jiangling and Chu tombs at Wangshan, Mashan, Baoshan in Jingmen, Guodian, and Jiuliandun in Zaoyang prove that Chu culture reached its heyday in Hubei. The discovery of a large quantity of heritages dating from the Qin and Han dynasties through the Tang and Song dynasties, together with the excavation of tombs of Ming feudal princes such as Prince Chuzhao, Prince Yingjing and Prince Liangzhuang, has enriched data for the study of local history and culture.

Hubei Provincial Museum is designed to protect, collect and display cultural heritages in the province. It was founded in the form of a preparatory office in March

1953, which was moved to Donghu scenic area, its present location, in the spring of 1959. It was officially named Hubei Provincial Museum in January 1963, when a 3,000-square-meter exhibition building was completed and opened to the public. In January 1999, the Exhibition Hall for Set-bells, which covers a floor space of 5,717 square meters, was opened. In December 2005, the Exhibition Hall for Chu Culture was opened. In September 2007, the new Comprehensive Exhibition Hall was opened. At present, the museum covers a total area of 81,909 square meters and a floor space of 49,611 square meters. Its exhibition halls cover a floor space of 13,427 square meters. It has a collection of more than 140,000 pieces (sets) of cultural heritages, among which there are nearly 1,000 pieces (sets) of first-grade cultural relics, ranking high among all provincial museums in China in this regard.

As the new Comprehensive Exhibition Hall opened, based on characteristics of our collection, we replaced our general-history exhibition with eleven theme exhibitions:

Yunxian Man: Prehistoric People in the Middle Reaches of the Yangtze, centering on the discovery of Yunxian Man fossils (treasure of the collection) and covering the discoveries of other Paleolithic heritages in Hubei, with supplementary information about the origin of the early man from all over the world, presents a general picture of the life of the early man.

Qujialing: Prehistoric Culture in the Middle Reaches of the Yangtze, tracing upward to Chengbeixi Culture dating from over 8,000 years ago and downward to Shijiahe Culture dating from 4,000 years ago, reveals the birth of Neolithic agriculture in the middle reaches of the Yangtze as well as the advent of settled life and civilization.

Panlongcheng: Bronze Civilization in the Middle Reaches of the Yangtze, which displays archaeological finds from the Panlongcheng site in Huangpi, the southern outpost of the Shang Dynasty, proves that the existence of copper resources at Tonglüshan, Daye, prompted the Shang culture to go south, which objectively contributed to civilization in the middle reaches of the Yangtze.

Tomb of Marquis Yi of Zeng is one of the best exhibitions offered by the museum. It has been expanded in area and increased in number of exhibits in order to show a complete picture of the rite-and-music culture in the times of Marquis Yi.

Records on Jiuliandun concentrates on the process of archaeological excavation and the burial culture reflected by tombs of senior nobles of Chu.

The Art of Lacquered Articles in the Qin and Han Dynasties, which displays the most characteristic Qin and Han lacquered articles collected by the museum, focuses mainly on techniques and artistic features.

Writing History: Bamboo Slips of the Warring States Period, the Qin Dynasty and the Han Dynasty is a pilot project for similar exhibitions in the future. Displaying bamboo slips, wooden tablets and writing tools unearthed in Hubei and tracing back to primitive engraved signs and pottery inscriptions, with supplementary information about the evolution of writing in other parts of the world, it offers visitors a comprehensive introduction to the history of writing.

The Art of Earth and Fire: Ancient Porcelain, focusing on celadon, blue-and-white porcelain and official-kiln porcelain, displays the best porcelain articles collected by Hubei Provincial Museum.

Tomb of Prince Liangzhuang: Treasure of the Era of Zheng He shows heritages unearthed from the Ming tomb of Prince Liangzhuang.

Ming and Qing Paintings and Calligraphic Works Collected by Hubei Provincial Museum features works by representative painters or calligraphers in the Ming and Qing dynasties.

Outstanding Figures over a Century in Hubei features stories of revolutionaries, historical figures and elites in culture, science and education from Hubei or working in Hubei for a long time, who were outstanding in their impact on or contribution to the history, science, culture or economic development of China in modern times. Therefore, these famous persons would be remembered for ever.

These exhibitions present highlights in the history and culture of Hubei from different perspectives, and outline the past of Hubei by various cultural heritages. Thus visitors have access to admire the wisdom of our ancestors while the museum becomes a valuable platform for intelligent dialogues and exchanges.

A series of albums has been published to meet the needs of the exhibitions. Each album contains an article written by an expert, which either gives brief information to the cultural background or concentrates on the cultural significance. The main part consists of pictures of cultural heritages with simple illustrations. They are generally designed to provide easy access to in-depth knowledge of the local history and culture in Hubei.

Curator of Hubei Provincial Museum
Director of Hubei Provincial Institute of Cultural Relics and Archaeology
Director of Center for Protection of Cultural Relics in Hubei

Wang Hongxing

长江中游旧石器时代考古概述

李天元

长江中游地区地貌类型复杂，生态环境优越，非常适合于人类生活。考古发现的资料证明，早在100多万年前，远古先民就在这块土地上生息劳作，创造了古朴而又灿烂的古代文化。

古人类学研究的成果证明，人类起源于一种进步的古猿类——南方古猿非洲种。大体经过了能人、直立人、早期智人和晚期智人等几个发展阶段，演化成为现代人。人类的历史有200万－300万年。300万年前处于古猿阶段。

1. 建始发现的魁人

1968年，中国科学院古脊椎动物与古人类研究所在湖北巴东县药材公司收购的"龙骨"中，发现了200多枚巨猿牙齿和1枚高等灵长类牙齿化石。其产地可能在相邻的建始县。1970年，对建始县高坪镇龙骨洞进行发掘，在地层堆积物中发现了哺乳动物化石，其中有5枚巨猿牙齿和3枚高等灵长类的牙齿化石。有学者认为这是南方古猿的[1]，也有学者认为是直立人的，可能是与能人相似的种类[2]。

1998－2000年对高坪龙骨洞进行了三次发掘，发现3枚人类牙齿和一批石制品。3枚牙齿是右上第

湖北旧石器时代重要遗址分布示意图

A map of the paleolithic sites in Hubei

三前臼齿（编号PA1278）、左上第三臼齿（编号PA1279）和右下第一臼齿（编号PA1277）。从牙齿的磨蚀程度看，很可能属于三个不同的个体。研究者将其归为人科，魁人属，古爪哇魁人种[3]。

学者们认为，关于"魁人"的归属问题，南方古猿类、能人和直立人的可能性都存在。更多材料的发现也许有利于破解"魁人"之谜。

从建始龙骨洞地层中获得592件石制品。其中石核73件，石片46件，石器189件，其余284件为石块和碎屑。石器类型简单，以刮削器为主，有177件，占石器总数的93.7%。石器加工粗糙，刃缘不平直，重量超过100克的标本很少，文化遗物与砾石石器文化遗存有明显的差别。

龙骨洞动物群包括小哺乳动物4个目，52种；大哺乳动物5个目，35种，具有浓厚的巫山龙骨坡动物群的时代特色。龙骨洞的巫山鼠比龙骨坡的显得进步，因而时代要晚。龙骨洞大哺乳动物群的时代早于柳州笔架山，晚于柳城巨猿洞。研究者根据动物群对比国际标准磁性年表，认为古人类化石层位时代早于215万年。

2. 郧县人和郧县人文化

江汉地区发现的直立人化石中，时代最早、材料最完整的当属"郧县人"。

1989年5月，郧县博物馆王正华等到郧县青曲镇弥陀寺村进行文物调查，在曲远河口学堂梁子发现1件古人类头骨化石（编号EV9001）。次年6月，对学堂梁子进行正式考古发掘，发现1件保存更为完好的古人类头骨化石（编号EV9002），同时还发现一批石制品和丰富的哺乳动物化石，据此确认学堂梁子是一处古人类遗址。

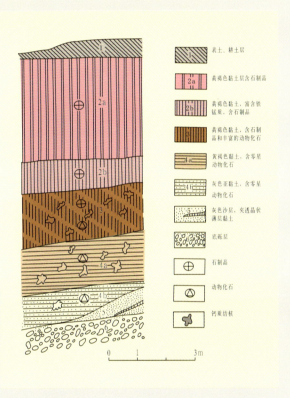

郧县人遗址地层剖面图 Geological strata of the Yunxian Man site

图例：
表土、耕土层
黄褐色黏土层含石制品
黄褐色黏土，富含铁锰质，含石制品
黄褐色黏土，含石制品和丰富的动物化石
黄褐色黏土，含零星动物化石
灰色亚黏土，含零星动物化石
灰色沙层，夹透晶状薄层黏土
底砾层
石制品
动物化石
钙质结核

0   1   3m

学堂梁子是汉江左岸的四级台地，顶部地面距汉江水面相对高程约50米。台地为土状堆积，厚13－17米，从上至下可分为6层。郧县人头骨化石出土于第3层。在第2、3、4层出土一批石制品。在第3、4、5层出土约2000件哺乳动物化石。

人类头骨化石虽然在地层中受到挤压而变形，但基本的形态特征很明显：颅顶低矮；眉脊粗厚，向两侧伸展；前额低平，向后倾斜；颅骨最宽位置在耳孔上方；枕骨不像现代人那样圆隆呈球形，而是有明显转折，枕骨圆枕（水平方向的一条凸棱）粗壮；吻部明显向前凸出；牙齿粗壮硕大，臼齿特别宽大。两件头骨都保留了很多的原始特征，与亚

郧县人 Ⅰ 号头骨化石 Yunxian Man Cranium Ⅰ

洲已经发现的直立人化石（如北京人、蓝田人、爪哇人等）的形态特征基本一致。郧县人属于直立人类型，定名为直立人郧县亚种，简称为"郧县人"。

从郧县人遗址获得493件石制品，其中石器92件。石器中以砾石加工的砍砸器为主要类型，共57件；其次为刮削器，26件；其他类型的石器数量很少：薄刃斧3件，石锤3件，单面器、两面器和雕刻器各1件。

石制品多为粗大的河滩砾石：石核和砍砸器全部为砾石制品。17件刮削器以砾石石片加工而成，占刮削器的65.38%；遗址中出土可拼合标本24组共55件，其中23组53件为砾石制品，占96.36%。打片和加工多采用锤击法。石器加工粗糙，多为单面加工，两面加工的很少。刃缘多不平直。石器类型简单，其中最有特点的器物是向心石核和郧县砍砸器。这一新的文化类型被命名为"郧县人文化"。郧县人文化是中国砾石石器文化遗存的早期代表。

与郧县人化石伴出的哺乳动物化石有23种，主要有蓝田金丝猴、裴氏猫、爪哇豺、桑氏鬣狗、大熊猫武陵山亚种、似剑齿虎、东方剑齿象、云南马、中国犀、中国貘、李氏野猪、小猪、秀丽黑鹿、云南水鹿、大角鹿、短角丽牛、水牛等。整个动物群具有南北方混合的色彩：大熊猫、东方剑齿

象、中国犀、中国貘、小猪、水牛是华南更新世"大熊猫—剑齿象动物群"的典型种类，裴氏猫、李氏野猪、秀丽黑鹿、大角鹿、短角丽牛则属于北方类型。更新世中期，秦岭山脉剧烈抬升，阻碍了动物南北的自由迁徙，这一时期，秦岭南麓和北麓动物群属种分布比较单一，都没有发现南、北方动物群混合的现象。由此可以推断，郧县人动物群生活在更新世早期。

古地磁测年表明，郧县人遗址地层剖面的地质年代为170万－70万年。第3和第4岩性层的年代是90万－83万年。对该遗址出土的动物牙齿釉质层进行电子自旋共振（ESR）测年，结果表明平均年龄大约为58万年。与古地磁测年结果比较，ESR测年结果明显偏低，原因可能是动物牙齿中铀含量达到饱和，影响了测年结果。地层的实际年龄应该与古地磁年龄接近。

将郧县人动物群和蓝田公王岭动物群进行对比，相同和相似属种达到60%以上，二者性质一致，所处的时代相同。郧县人遗址的年代当为早更新世晚期，距今约100万年。

3. 洞庭湖区的砾石石器文化遗存

洞庭湖区旧石器遗址点多分布在西部的沅水中游和澧水流域。东部湘水和资水流域目前发现的地点少且分散，文化面貌还不很清楚。西部的遗址点主要是砾石石器文化遗存，研究者将其区分为舞水文化类群和澧水文化类群。

舞水文化类群主要分布在舞水、渠水和沅水河谷地带。打片和加工方法以锤击法为主，也常用锐棱砸击法，间或使用碰砧法。尖刃、长身侧刃、双边刃和端刃砍砸器是这个类群很有特点的器物。澧水文化类群主要分布在澧水流域和洞庭湖西岸的平原地区。打片与加工方法以锤击法为主，偶尔采用碰砧法。典型器物有大石片、各种形式的大尖状

器、似手斧石器和石球等。早中期器物形体较大，晚期小型石器数量增多[4]。

4. 长阳人和石龙头文化

大约在距今30万年，人类发展为智人阶段。早期智人以长阳人为代表。

1956年在长阳县下钟家湾发现人类化石，以其产地命名为"长阳人"。化石材料有1件残破的左侧上颌骨（保存有第一前臼齿和第一臼齿），还有1枚单独的左下第二前臼齿。上颌骨和牙齿保留了一定的原始性状，同时具备较多的进步特征，属于早期智人类型。与长阳人伴生的动物化石种类有豪猪、古豺、大熊猫、中国鬣狗、东方剑齿象、巨貘、中国犀、牛、鹿等，属于华南广义的"大熊猫—剑齿象动物群"。该动物群生活的时代属更新世的中、晚期，对动物牙齿取样进行铀系法测年研究的结果为距今19万年。

1971年在大冶章山石龙头发现一处旧石器时代遗址，出土了88件石制品。1986年在宜都县（今枝城市）九道河一处石灰岩裂隙中发掘出近400件石制品。石制品原料均为砾石。剥片以锤击法为主，偶尔采用砸击法。石核以天然台面为主，有少量人工台面标本，没有发现修理台面的标本。石器加工以单面打击为主，偶尔有异向打击的小块片疤。石器加工粗糙，只有砍砸器和刮削器两类。石龙头和九道河的文化遗存性质一致，同属于砾石石器文化遗存，与华南常见的砾石石器文化遗存又略有区别，因之命名为"石龙头文化"。两个地点发现的动物化石都属于华南广义的"大熊猫—剑齿象动物群"，时代为晚更新世早期。北京大学考古学系对长阳人地点和大冶石龙头进行铀系测年的结果为：前者距今约19万年，后者略大于19万年。这三个地点处于同一时代，创造石龙头文化的人类应是与长阳人同时代的早期智人。

清江流域也是研究人类起源和发展的重要地区之一。除了上述发现的建始古爪哇魁人和长阳人之外，还发现伴峡小洞、榨洞和鲢鱼山等遗址。在伴峡小洞发现一批石制品，还发现有用火遗迹；鲢鱼山也发现有用火遗迹。它们的年代为距今13万—10万年。

5. 晚期智人及其文化

大约在距今5万年前，人类进入到晚期智人阶段。晚期智人在形态特征方面保留有较少的原始性状，与现代人没有明显的区别。晚期智人在地域上分布很广，世界各地都有化石材料发现。在长江中游地区发现晚期智人化石的地点有湖南石门燕儿洞，湖北郧西黄龙洞、长阳果酒岩、武汉市汉南区汉阳纱帽山。石器地点数十处，重要的遗址和地点有江陵鸡公山、丹江口石鼓、房县樟脑洞等。

黄龙洞位于湖北省郧西县，是一个石灰岩溶洞。2004年在漫川高速公路修建时，在这里发现5枚古人类牙齿化石，石化程度很轻，保存基本完整，特征清楚，与现代人牙齿没有明显区别，属于晚期智人类型。伴生哺乳动物化石48种，多为南方"大熊猫—剑齿象动物群"中较常见的种类。绝灭种类有最后鬣狗、巴氏大熊猫、东方剑齿象、中国犀、巨貘等，时代为更新世晚期。地层中还出土数量不多但制作较精致的石器，属旧石器时代晚期。

汉阳人头骨发现于武汉市汉南区纱帽镇长江江滩上，保存了额骨和基本完整的左右侧顶骨。枕骨自人字缝脱失。石化程度很深。额骨和顶骨较隆起。头骨最宽位置较高，在顶结节下方。颅内脑膜中动脉分支清晰，较简单。汉阳人头骨已经脱失地层，无法判断时代。头骨周边未见磨蚀痕迹，说明没有经过流水远距离搬运。对汉阳人头骨进行追踪调查，头骨发现地点在汉阳纱帽山下游约300米处。纱帽山为一处商周古文化遗址，其文化层底部有一条含有更新世沉积物的褐红色古土壤层，里面发现1件旧石器时代的砂岩砾石石核。汉阳人头骨是否出土于产石核的古土壤层，还有待今后的工作来证实。

江陵鸡公山是一处旧石器时代遗址，下文化层大致处在旧石器时代晚期的较早阶段。在当时人类的活动面上遗留有石片、废片、碎屑和各类石器上万件。文化属性为砾石工业遗存。打制石器的原料为砾石，成分比较复杂。发掘者做过小范围的单位统计，所出土约200件的标本中，石英岩约占38%，

以石片石器为主。年代测定为距今1.35万年，处在旧石器时代晚期之末。在文化比较发达的地区，有可能已经进入新石器时代。

6. 结语

长江中游地区地形复杂，气候温和，自然条件适宜于古人类生活。郧县人是生活在这一地区时代很早的直立人，他们创造的郧县人文化，是中国砾石石器文化遗存的早期代表之一。砾石石器文化遗存从旧石器时代早期一直延续到晚期，存在着地区差异和时代差异，但文化内涵的主体因素是一致的。江陵鸡公山是砾石石器文化遗存的晚期代表之一。

到了旧石器时代晚期，文化面貌发生变化。除了鸡公山一类砾石石器文化遗存之外，有很多地点的文化遗存以中小型石片石器为主，如房县樟脑洞、丹江口石鼓。在房县和湖南境内的有些地点还发现以细小石器为主的遗存（有的学者称之为"细石器"，其实是与细石器文化遗存有区别的细小石器）。在此期间，新的文化因素逐渐在孕育、在积累，达到质的飞跃的时候，就进入到一个全新的时代——新石器时代。

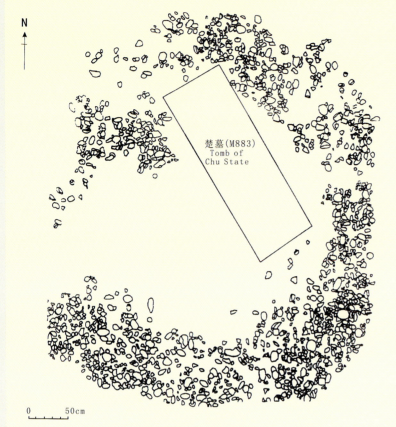

江陵鸡公山遗址发现的大石圈遗迹
Distribution of stone tools on Jigongshan, Jiangling

（楚墓(M883)
Tomb of
Chu State

0   50cm）

其次为火成岩，约占31%，石英砂岩约占22%，砂岩为4%，燧石和脉石英数量很少。石器类型有常见的砍砸器、尖状器和刮削器等。大尖状器最具特色，加工方法固定，形制比较一致。在活动面上还发现有石圈遗迹。小石圈为直径1.5－1.8米的椭圆形，大石圈直径在2－2.5米之间。有学者认为小石圈可能是打制石器的场所，大石圈可能是与当时的人类居住有关的遗迹。

房县樟脑洞是一处旧石器时代洞穴遗址。从樟脑洞获得2000余件石制品。原料以脉石英和黑色硅质岩为主，各占约40%，砂岩约占15%。石制品的加工也比较简单，打片以锤击法为主，间或使用砸击法。第二步加工的方法较为多样，就一条刃缘而论，单面加工为主。遗物中石片占很大比例，石器

注释

[1] 高建：《与鄂西巨猿共生的南方古猿牙齿化石》，《古脊椎动物与古人类》1975年第13卷第2期。

[2] 张银运：《鄂西"南方古猿"和印尼早更新世若干人类化石》，《人类学学报》1984年第3卷第2期。

[3] 郑绍华：《建始人遗址》，科学出版社，2004年。

[4] 袁家荣：《湖南旧石器文化的区域性类型及其地位》，《长江中游史前文化暨第二届亚洲文明学术讨论会论文集》，岳麓书社，1996年。

湖北发现的古人类一览表
Hominid of Hubei Province

年代 Time period	县/地点 County/Locality	古人类分类 Hominid taxon	化石标本 Fossil specimens	发现时间 Discovery time
早更新世早期 Early stage of Lower Pleistocene	建始巨猿洞 Jianshi, Juyuandong	魁人 *Meganthropus*	牙齿3 Tooth 3	1999－2000
早更新世晚期 Late stage of Lower Pleistocene	郧县曲远河口 Yun county, Quyuan river mouth	直立人 *Homo erectus*	头骨2 Cranium 2	1989 1990
中更新世 Middle Pleistocene	郧县龙骨洞 Yun county, Longgudong		牙齿4 Tooth 4	1975
	郧西白龙洞 Yunxi, Bailongdong		牙齿7 Tooth 7	1976
	建始龙骨洞 Jianshi, Longgudong		牙齿3 Tooth 3	1970
晚更新世早期 Early stage of Upper Pleistocene	长阳龙骨洞 Changyang, Longgudong	早期智人 Early *Homo sapiens*	上颌骨1、牙齿1 Maxilla 1, Tooth 1	1956 1957
晚更新世晚期 Late stage of Upper Pleistocene	长阳果酒岩 Changyang, Guojiuyan	晚期智人 Late *Homo sapiens*	部分头骨、颚骨残片、肱骨12、头骨残片7 Partial cranium, jawbone fragments, distal humerus12, post-cranial fragments 7	1982
	郧西黄龙洞 Yunxi, Huanglongdong		牙齿5 Tooth 5	2004
	汉阳纱帽山 Hanyang, Shamaoshan		头骨残片1 Cranium 1	1997

● 湖北地区发现的旧石器时代文化遗址有数十处，在长江流域是古人类发生序列最为完整的。其中晚期直立人、早期智人和晚期智人的化石均有发现。此外，在建始还发现有人类旁支巨猿化石。

● Dozens of Paleolithic cultural sites have been discovered in Hubei, which has the most complete array of remains attesting to the evolution of ancient human being in the valley of the Yangtze. Discovered fossils include those of late *Homo erectus*, early *Homo sapiens*, and late *Homo sapiens*. In Jianshi were discovered fossils of *Gigantopithecus*, a human-related species.

Summary of Paleolithic Archaeology in the Middle Reaches of the Yangtze
Li Tianyuan

Archaeological finds in the middle reaches of the Yangtze indicate that the region was populated by man over a million years ago.

As proved by paleoanthropological researches, the human species originated from *Australopithecus africanus*, and evolved into modern man through the following stages: *Homo habilis*, *Homo erectus*, early *Homo sapiens* and late *Homo sapiens.*

1. *Meganthropus* discovered in Jianshi

In 1968, archaeologists from Institute of Vertebrate Paleontology and Paleoanthropology, Chinese Academy of Sciences, discovered in Badong more than 200 *Gigantopithecus* teeth and one tooth fossil of higher primates. In 1970, the excavation of Longgudong in Gaoping Town, Jianshi County revealed five *Gigantopithecus* teeth and three tooth fossils of higher primates, which were believed to belong to *Australopithecus* or *Homo erectus*. During the 1998-2000 period, three human teeth and a number of stone artifacts were discovered. The teeth were found to represent *Meganthropus palaeojavanicus* in the genus of *Meganthropus* in the family of Hominidae.

Stone tools obtained from geological layers of Longgudong in Jianshi are simple, with scrapers being predominant. They were crudely made, with edges that are not straight. There are few specimens that weigh over 100 grams. The cultural remains differ widely from remains of Pebble Stone Culture.

Fauna of Longgudong included small mammals of 52 species in four orders, and large mammals of 35 species in five orders. Comparison of fauna indicates that the fossils of *Gigantopithecus* date from about 2.15 million years ago.

2. Yunxian Man and its culture

In May 1989, one hominid cranium (EV 9001) was discovered at Xuetangliangzi at the mouth of Quyuan River. In June 1990, excavation formally started here and revealed one better preserved cranium fossil (EV 9002).

The crania have the following features: low calvaria, thick brow ridge extending to both sides; low and flat forehead reclining backwards; the widest part of the skull being above the ear hole; obvious bending in occipital; obviously protruding lips; large, sturdy teeth. These are in substantial agreement with the features of fossils *Homo erectus* (e.g. Peking Man, Lantian Man and Java Man) discovered in Asia. Yunxian Man, a subspecies of *Homo erectus*, is named *H. e. yunxianensis.*

A total of 493 stone artifacts were obtained at the Yunxian Man site. Most of them are made of large pebbles collected at the river bank. All the stone cores and choppers are made of pebbles. 17 scrapers are made of pebble flakes, accounting for 65.38% of all scrapers. There are 55 conjoined specimens in twenty-four groups, 96.36% of which are made of pebbles. Hammering was usually used for chipping and processing. The stone tools were crudely processed, mostly on one side only, with edges that are not straight. Their types are simple, the most characteristic tools being centripetal cores and Yunxian choppers. This new type of culture was named Yunxian Man Culture.

Fossils of 23 mammal species were unearthed together with the Yunxian Man fossils. Major species are: *Rhinopithecus lantianensis*, *Felis peii*, *Ailuropoda melanoleuca wulingshanensis*, *Homotherium*, *Stegodon orientalis*, *Sus lydekkeri*, *Sus xiaozhu*, *Cervus elegans*, and *Leptobos brovicornis*. *Ailuropoda* and *Stegodon orientalis* were typical of the 'Ailuropoda-Stegodon fauna' in South China in Pleistocene, while *Felis peii*, *Sus lydekkeri* and *Cervus elegans* were northern species. In the mid Pleistocene, Qinling Mountain Range rose sharply, blocking the way for animals to move freely between the south and the north. At that time, fauna at the southern and northern foot of Qinling was rather homogeneously distributed, with no sign of such mingling of southern and northern species. From this it could be concluded that the fauna living with Yunxian Man existed in the early Pleistocene.

Paleomagnetic dating indicates that Yunxian Man site dates from 1.7 million-0.7 million years ago, and that the third and fourth rocky layers date from 900,000-830,000 years ago. Species of Yunxian-Man fauna was over 60% identical or similar to those of the fauna at Gongwangling, Lantian; they were of the same characteristics and dated from the same period. It is concluded that Yunxian Man site dates from the late

period of early Pleistocene about 1 million years ago.

3. Pebble Stone Culture remains in the Basin of Dongting Lake

Paleolithic sites in the Basin of Dongting Lake are mostly distributed in the middle reaches of Yuanshui River in the west and in the valley of Lishui River. Sites in the west mostly contain remains of Pebble Stone Culture, which were divided into Wushui Culture Group and Lishui Culture Group.

In Wushui Culture Group, hammering was mainly used for chipping and processing; typical tools are those with pointed blades, those with long bodies and side blades, those with double edges and those with end edges. In Lishui Culture Group, hammering was mainly used for chipping and processing, and colliding was occasionally used.

4. Changyang Man and Shilongtou Culture

Man evolved into *Homo sapiens* about 300,000 years ago. Changyang Man is typical of early *Homo sapiens*.

In 1956, one broken left maxillae and one molar fossil belonging to early *Homo sapiens* were discovered at Xiazhongjiawan in Changyang County. Samples of tooth fossils of accompanied animals coexisting with Changyang Man fossils were uranium-series dated back to 190,000 years ago.

In 1971, a Paleolithic site was discovered at Shilongtou, Zhangshan, Daye, where 88 stone artifacts were unearthed. In 1986, nearly 400 stone artifacts

were unearthed at Jiudaohe site in Yidu County. The stone tools were crudely processed, mostly on one side only. They fall into only two categories—choppers and scrapers. Cultural remains at Shilongtou and those at Jiudaohe, both dating back to a little more than 190,000 years ago, are remains of Pebble Stone Culture, but differ a little from those commonly found in south China. The culture they represent was named Shilongtou Culture.

The Valley of Qingjiang River was also one of the important areas for studying the origin and evolution of man. Apart from *Meganthropus palaeojavanicus* discovered in Jianshi and Changyang Man, other sites such as Banxiaxiaodong, Zhadong and Lianyushan were discovered, which date from 130,000-100,000 years ago.

5. Late *Homo sapiens* and its culture

Man evolved into late *Homo sapiens* about 50,000 years ago. Fossils of late *Homo sapiens* were discovered at Shimen Yan'erdong in Hunan, Huanglongdong in Yunxi, Guojiuyan in Changyang, and Shamaoshan of Hanyang, Hannan District in Wuhan (the last three are in Hubei). Dozens of stone tool sites were discovered, important ones of which include Jigongshan in Jiangling, Shigu at the mouth of Danjiang River, and Zhangnaodong in Fang County.

Five hominid tooth fossils were discovered at Huanglongdong. Petrified to a low degree and largely integral, with clearly visible features, they are not much different from teeth of modern man, belonging to the late *Homo sapiens*. A small number of exquisitely made

stone tools were unearthed from geological layers, which date from the late Paleolithic Age.

The cranium of Hanyang Man was discovered on the riverside of the Yangtze at Shamao Town in Hannan District, Wuhan. It retains the frontal bone and largely integral left and right parietal bones. The part of the occipital below sutura lambdoidea has been lost. The cranium is petrified to a high degree. The frontal bone and the parietal bones bulge rather obviously. The widest part of the skull is located rather high, below parietal tuber. Shamaoshan in Hanyang, where the cranium was discovered, is a site of Shang and Zhou culture, in which was discovered one Paleolithic sandstone core. Whether the cranium of Hanyang Man was unearthed from the paleosol layer which produced cores needs to be testified in the future.

Jigongshan in Jiangling is a Paleolithic site. Its bottom cultural layer roughly dates from the early period of the late Paleolithic Age, about 50,000 years ago. About ten thousand remains—stone flakes, waste flakes, crumbs and various types of stone tools—are found on the layer of human activities. Chipped stone tools were made of pebbles in a complex variety. There are such common types as choppers, points and scrapers. The most characteristic are large points, which are nearly uniform in shape and size.

Zhangnaodong in Fang County is a Paleolithic cave site, where more than 2,000 stone artifacts were obtained. They are mainly made of vein quartz and black silicalite, each accounting for about 40%; sandstone accounts for 15%. They were simply processed, with hammering, and occasionally striking, used for chipping off flakes. The majority of them are flakes. They are dated back to 13,500 years ago, at the end of late Paleolithic Age.

6. Conclusion

The middle reaches of the Yangtze was suitable for hominid to live. Yunxian Man was a very early species of *Homo erectus* living in the region. Yunxian Man Culture is one of the typical early Pebble Stone Cultures in China. Pebble Stone Culture remains, dating from the early through the late Paleolithic Age, are consistent in major cultural contents despite regional and temporal differences. Jigongshan, Jiangling is one of the typical sites among late pebble culture remains.

我们是谁

100万年前，我们生活在今天的郧县曲远河口一带。在曲远河与汉江交汇处有一块可供我们生活的高台地。后来阶地不断抬升，这里变成山岗。现代居民在此建有弥陀寺小学，这条山岗就称被为学堂梁子。我们的遗骸在地层中埋藏了100万年之久。

1989年5月，第一个头骨化石被发现（编为1号头骨，EV9001）。一年之后又发现了II号头骨化石（EV9002）。头骨化石因地层堆积物挤压变形，颅顶低平，牙齿粗壮。有的人类学家认为我们属于直立人，有的认为属于早期智人。我们到底处在人类进化的哪一个阶段？

Who Were We?

A million years ago, we lived near the mouth of Quyuan River in the present-day Yunxian, on an elevated piece of land where Quyuan River meets Hanshui River. The place later rose into a hill. After a primary school was built on it, the hill became known as Xuetangliangzi. Our remains were buried here for a million years.

In May 1989, the first cranium fossil was discovered (Cranium I, EV 9001); a year later Cranium II was discovered (EV 9002). Deformed by geological sediments, the crania have low and flat tops and thick, sturdy teeth. Some anthropologists believe that we were a species of *Homo erectus*, while some say that we belonged to early *Homo sapiens*. At what stage of the human evolution did we exist?

我们生活的自然环境
Our Living Environment

学堂梁子位于汉江左岸、曲远河汇入汉江的河口。梁子为汉江的第四级阶地。第一级阶地为高出河水面5－8米的漫滩。第二级阶地是钙质胶结的沙层，高出河水面15－18米。第三级阶地是沙质黏土覆盖的沙砾层，胶结坚硬，高出河水面25－30米。第四级阶地高出河水面约50米，为基座型阶地。基岩上的土层厚12－20米。当时森林茂密，我们就生活在第四级阶地上。

Xuetangliangzi is located on the left bank of Hanshui River, where Quyuan River converges into Hanshui River. It is the fourth terrace of the Hanshui River. The first terrace is a floodplain 5 to 8 meters above the river; the second terrace, a sand stratum composed of calcareous cementation; the third terrace, a stratum of cemented grit covered by sandy clay 25 to 30 meters above the river; the fourth terrace, a base-type terrace some 50 meters above the river, with a 12-20-meter-thick layer of earth on bedrocks. We lived on the fourth terrace, at a time when it was covered by a dense forest.

郧县人头骨化石发现地曲远河口学堂梁子（由南向北）
Xuetangliangzi at the mouth of Quyuan River, where the fossils of
Yunxian Man crania were discovered (from south to north)

郧县人头骨化石发现地曲远河口学堂梁子（由西向东，中间石碑为发现头骨地点）
Xuetangliangzi at the mouth of Quyuan River, where the fossils of
Yunxian Man crania were discovered(from west to east).The stone
tablets indicate the places where the crania were discovered.

我们的动物伙伴
Animals Sharing Our Habitat

在学堂梁子这个亚热带森林的边缘，和我们在一起生活的动物包括6个目（啮齿、长鼻、灵长、食肉、奇蹄、偶蹄），26个种，既有北方属种的裴氏猫、李氏野猪、大角鹿、秀丽黑鹿、短角丽牛等，也有华南"大熊猫—剑齿象动物群"的属种，如武陵山大熊猫、东方剑齿象、中国犀、中国貘、云南马、小猪、麂、水牛等。既有第三纪的残留种，如似剑齿虎，也有早更新世的典型种类，如蓝田金丝猴、桑氏鬣狗、武陵山大熊猫、秀丽黑鹿、云南水鹿等，证明我们生活的时代早到早更新世晚期，距今约100万年。

We shared Xuetangliangzi, a habitat on the verge of a subtropical forest, with animals of 26 species in 6 orders (*Rodentia*, *Proboscidea*, primates, *Carnivora*, *Perissodactyla* and *Artiodactyla*). There were northern species (*Felis peii*, *Sus lydekkeri*, *Megaloceros*, *Cervus elegans* and *Leptobos brevicornis*), southern panda-*Stegodon* assemblages (*Ailuropoda melanoleuca wulingshanensis*, *Stegodon orientalis*, *Rhinoceros sinensis*, *Tapirus sinensis*, *Equus yunnanensis*, *Sus xiaozhu*, *Muntiacus* and buffaloes, species remaining from Tertiary (*Homotherium*), and species typical of Early Pleistocene (*Rhinopithecus lantianensis*, *Hyaena licenti*, *Ailuropoda melanoleuca wulingshanensis*, *Cervus elegans*, and *Ruas yunnanensis*). Their presence indicates that human beings lived as early as in the late Early Pleistocene, about one million years ago.

蓝田金丝猴
Rhinopithecus lantianensis Gu et Jeblonski

中国貘
Tapirus sinensis Owen

虎
Panthera tigris L.

小猪
Sus xiaozhu Han, Xu et Yi

爪哇豺
Cuon javanicus Desmarest

桑氏鬣狗
Hyaena licenti Pei

秀丽黑鹿
Cervus elegans Teilhard et Piveteau

短角丽牛
Leptobos brevicornis Hu
et Qi

中国黑熊头骨化石
Ursus thibetanus Cuvier

高10、长25.5、宽13cm

中国貘头骨化石
Tapirus sinensis Owen

高16、长43、宽20cm

裴氏猫上颌骨化石
Felis peii Teilhard

高7、长15.5、宽8cm

中国犀下牙床化石
Rhinoceros sinensis Owen

高8、长18、宽4cm

考古人员在郧县人发掘现场清理动物骨骼化石
Archaeologists sorting out fossils of animal bones at the Yunxian Man site

郧县人遗址中出土的中国貘头骨化石
The fossils of *Tapirus sinensis* Owen unearthed
from the Yunxian Man site

直立人生活环境图
Living environment of *Homo erectus*

我们如何被发现?

How Were We Discovered?

1989年5月18日，郧县博物馆王正华和郧西县文化馆屈胜民到郧县曲远河口进行文物普查。他们根据线索到学堂梁子发掘出一件被胶结物包裹严实的头骨化石。该化石送到古人类学家贾兰坡教授那里，他反复观察化石后说："这是件国宝！"他注意到头骨有四个方面的特征：1.门齿着生陡直；2.犬齿不突出，前后没有齿隙；3.臼齿从前至后逐渐增大，第三臼齿尤其宽大；4.齿弓近似"U"形，似为南方古猿。1990年，对学堂梁子进行正式考古发掘，发现I号头骨化石的地点位于探方T745的北隔梁。6月15日，在同一探方的西壁深约110厘米处发现了II号头骨化石。

从修整后的头骨化石看，我们的形态特征均属直立人，被定名为"直立人郧县亚种"，简称"郧县人"。

On May 18, 1989, Wang Zhenghua from Museum of Yun County and Qu Shengmin from Cultural Center of Yunxi County were conducting a survey of cultural relics at the mouth of Quyuan River in Yun County. Based on clues, they went to Xuetangliangzi, where they discovered a cranium fossil entirely wrapped in cemented substance. They took it to Jia Lanpo, a professor on Paleoanthropology. Having observed it carefully, Jia exclaimed, 'This must be a national treasure!' He noticed four features: 1. The incisors are steep and straight; 2. The canines are not prominent, with no gaps between them and adjacent teeth; 3. The cheek teeth increase in size from front to back, with the third cheek tooth being especially wide; 4. The teeth are arranged in a quasi-U shape, similar to the teeth of *Australopithecus* sp. In 1990 an archaeological excavation was officially started at Xuetangliangzi. Cranium I was found at the northern balk of T745. On June 15, Cranium II was found about 110 cm underground under the western wall of T745.

Judging from the features of repaired fossils, we belonged to *Homo erectus*, and were named *Homo erectus yunxianensis*, which is abbreviated as Yunxian Man.

郧县人 I 号头骨化石
Yunxian Man Cranium I

颅高12，颅长26，颅宽19cm

郧县人 I 号头骨化石是湖北首次发现的最完整的古人类头骨化石。

郧县人 I 号头骨化石侧面
The profile of Yunxian Man Cranium I

郧县人 I 号头骨颅腔
The cranial cavity of Yunxian Man Cranium I

郧县人 Ⅱ 号头骨化石
Yunxian Man Cranium II

颅高11.9、颅长21.7、颅宽17cm

郧县人 Ⅱ 号头骨化石是目前我国保存最为完好的直立人头骨化石。

郧县人 长江中游的远古人类

郧县人 Ⅱ 号头骨化石侧面
The profile of Yunxian Man Cranium II

郧县人 Ⅱ 号头骨颅腔
The cranial cavity of Yanxian Man Cranium II

1989年文物普查时发现郧县人Ⅰ号头骨化石地点（红色箭头处）
Spot where Yunxian Man Cranium I was discovered during a cultural relics survey in 1989 (indicated by the red arrow)

郧县人Ⅱ号头骨化石的发现地点（红色箭头处）
Spot Where Yunxian Man Cranium II Was discovered (indicated by the red arrow)

1990年在郧县人遗址发掘现场
Site of the excavation of the Yunxian Man site in 1990

考古人员在郧县人Ⅰ号头骨化石处开挖的探方
Tanfang excavated by archaeologists at the place where Yunxian Man Cranium I was discovered

考古人员在郧县人化石发掘现场
Archaeologists at the site of the excavation of Yunxian Man fossils

地层中发现的化石
Fossils in geological strata

郧县人使用的石器　　Stone tools used by Yunxian Man

郧县人遗址发现的石制品共493件，其中石器和半成品417件,占84.58%；完整砾石76件，占15.42%。从郧县人遗址附近采集两面器4件，双刃砍砸器1件，双刃刮削器1件，共6件。石制工具和原料均为当地河滩砾石，加工地点就在郧县人遗址。

A total of 493 stone artifacts were found at the Yunxian Man site, including 417 (84.58%) finished and unfinished stone tools, and 76 (15.42%) complete pebbles. In the vicinity of the site were found four bifaces, one double-edge chopper and one scraper (6 in total). All tools are made of pebbles from the local river bank, and the locale for the processing was right at the site.

砍砸器
Choppers

最大：多刃砍砸器，长 26，宽14cm

最小：单刃砍砸器，长10.4，宽9.2cm

郧县人遗址共发现石器92件，其中砍砸器有57件，分为单刃、端刃、双刃、多刃和郧县砍砸器等类型。郧县人砍砸器最具特色。

郧县砍砸器
Yunxian chopper
长28.5，宽12cm

该砍砸器是单面加工边刃和端刃的长条形扁平砾石，他处所未见。

刮削器
Scrappers
最大：多刃刮削器，长14.7，宽10cm
最小：凹缺刮削器，长5.8，宽4.2cm

郧县人遗址出土刮削器有26件，分单刃、双刃、多刃、凹缺等多种。

石片
Stone flakes

最大：石英斑岩，长8.4，宽5.7cm
最小：脉石英，长2.5，宽2.1cm

郧县人遗址出土的石片有花岗斑岩、石英斑岩、燧石和脉石英等。

石核
Stone cores

最大：多台面石核，长13.2，宽12cm
最小：双台面石核，长7.3，宽6.5cm

石核即用来打制石片的砾石或石块。郧县人遗址发现石核83件，以在砾石周边打击，在同一个面剥取石片的向心石核。

特殊石器

Special stone tools

左1：两面器 Biface，长20.5、宽11.3cm

左2：两面器 Biface，长22.5、宽10.7cm

左3：薄刃斧 Thin—edged axe，长14.3、宽10.3cm

左4：雕刻器 Burin，长11、宽6.5cm

薄刃斧为燧石砾石，两面加工。郧县人遗址出土薄刃斧共2件。

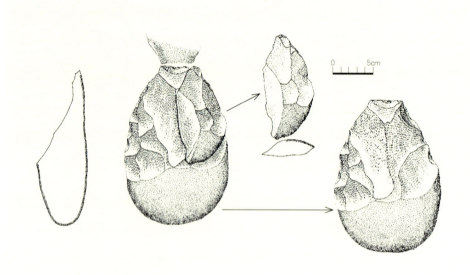

拼合标本

Conjoined specimen

单面器：长20.5、宽14.5cm

石片：长12.7、宽6.5cm

郧县人遗址出土可拼合的石器标本共24组55件，分为石片与石片、石核与石片、碎片与石片、碎块与碎块及石器与石片的五类拼合。它们证实该地点即为郧县人生活的原生地。

拼合标本

Conjoined specimen

通长9.5，宽9cm

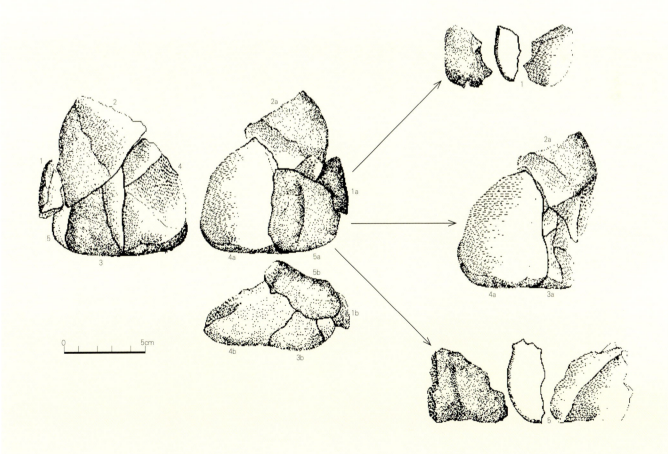

科学家对我们的研究
Scientists' Studies on Us

科学家对我们的研究分为人类化石、石制工具、动物群和年代学的研究。人类学家研究头骨化石是确定我们在人类进化中的位置。考古学家研究石器是探讨我们的生产技术水平。古生物学家研究动物群是推断我们的生存时代和生活环境。年代学研究是借助于技术手段，如古地磁、电子自旋共振（ESR）和铀系法测年等，推断我们的时代。综合这些研究结果，我们属于晚期直立人。

Scientists study us in terms of human fossils, stone tools, fauna and chronology. Anthropologists study the fossils of our crania to define our position in the evolution of mankind. Archaeologists study stone tools to learn our technological level. Paleontologists study the fauna to infer the age and environment in which we lived. Chronologists use such technological means as paleomagnetism, ESR and uranium series dating to infer our living times. A comprehensive study of the results indicates that we belonged to the late *Homo erectus*.

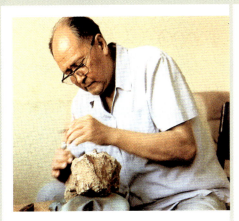

化石修理专家胡承志教授在武汉精心修理被钙质结核包裹的郧县人Ⅱ号头骨化石，修理后的化石显示出直立人的形态特征
Professor Hu Chengzhi restoring Yunxian Man Cranium II, which shows physical features of *Homo erectus*

1989年10月，贾兰坡院士在北京中国科学院古脊椎动物与古人类研究所观察郧县人Ⅰ号头骨化石
Academician Jia Lanpo observing Yunxian Man Cranium I at Institute of Vertebrate Paleontology and Paleoanthropology,Chinese Academy Sciences, in Beijing in October 1989

2000 年，中、法联合考古队在郧县人出土地点进行地质取样
In 2000, Sino-French archaeological team taking geological samples at the site where Yunxian Man fossils were unearthed

郧县人与直立人颅骨形态特征比较表
Between the Yunxian Man and the *Homo erectus*

序号 Serial number	直立人颅骨形态特征 Physical features of the cranium of *Homo erectus*	郧县人颅骨形态特征 Physical features of the cranium of Yunxian Man
1	颅骨较长，颅顶较低 Long skull and low calvarium	✓*
2	面部较宽而短 Wide and short face	✓
3	中上面较平 Flat upper-middle face	✓
4	眉脊粗壮 Thick brow ridge	✓
5	两外侧端较发达 Well-developed outer ends	眉间略向前凸 Slight protrusion between brows
	顶面观，眉脊呈一字形向两侧伸展 Brow ridge extends to both sides in a straight line	两侧略向后展 Outer ends slightly bend backward
6	眶不呈圆形，眶间宽较大 Eye sockets are not round, with wide gap between them	✓
7	鼻骨较宽 Wide nose bone	✓
8	梨状孔下缘界线不明显 Indistinct lower border of pyriform aperture	✓
9	额部明显向后倾斜 Evidently reclining brow	✓
10	有明显的眉脊上沟 Evident groove above brow ridge	明显但不深 Obvious but not deep
11	有明显的矢状脊和十字隆凸 Evident sagittal ridge and cruciform eminence	不明显 Unobvious
12	顶骨较短，顶骨弧较平 Short parietal bone, with slight curve	✓
13	没有枕外隆凸，该点与颅后点在同一位置 No external occipital protuberance, same position as opisthion	✓
14	枕平面与顶平面呈角状过渡，枕骨曲角较小 Angular transition between occipital plane and parietal plane, with occipital having small bending angle	✓
15	枕骨圆枕发达 Well-developed oceipital torus	✓

* 表示与左栏相同，下同。

16	枕平面短于顶平面，顶平面倾角较大 Occipital plane is shorter than parietal plane, which has a large obliquity	✓
17	颞骨鳞部较低，上缘较平直 Temporal bone has low pars squamosa and straight upper border	较高较长，上缘略呈凸弧形 Relatively high and long, with upper border slightly curved upward
18	乳突上脊发达，覆盖外耳门部分很深 Crista supramastoidea has been well-developed and deeply covers external acoustic foramen	✓
19	乳突脊发达 Well developed mastoid process ridge	✓
20	颅最大宽位于乳突上脊附近 Maximum-width points of skull are near crista supramastoidea	✓
21	乳突较小，乳突尖明显内收 Small mastoid process, with evidently retracted point	乳突较大 Relatively large mastoid process
22	鼓部轴与锥体轴夹角较大 Large angle between pars tympanica and conic axis	✓
23	下颌关节窝较窄而深 Narrow and deep acetabulum in mandible	✓
24	盂后突不明显 Unobvious postglenoid processus aborolis	✓
25	角圆枕显著 Prominent Torus angularis	不显著 Unobvious
26	脑容量较小 Small brain volume	脑容量较大 Relatively large brain volume

郧县人与北京猿人、大荔猿人头骨测量比较表
Measurement comparison on cranium between Yunxian Man, Peking Man and Dali Man

	北京人头骨(平均) Cranium of Peking Man (average)	大荔人头骨 Cranium of Dali Man	郧县人 II 号头骨 Yunxian Man Cranium II
颅长(S-op)	196.9mm	207mm	217.5mm
颅宽(cu-cu)	140.3mm	149mm	170mm
颅底点至前囟点高(ba-b)	115mm	118mm	119mm

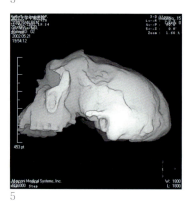

1

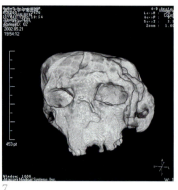

2

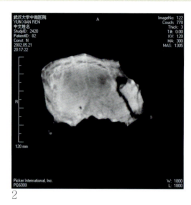

郧县人Ⅱ号头骨化石的计算机三维复原
Computer 3D reconstruction of Yunxian Man Cranium II

科技工作者在处理郧县人Ⅱ号头骨CT扫描图像
Scholar processing CT scanning image of Yunxian Man Cranium II

人类头骨脑容量研究在古人类研究中有决定性的意义。"郧县人"头骨化石因挤压变形造成研究困难。我国科学家采用CT扫描方式对Ⅱ号头骨化石进行图像的二维和三维重建，后又与法国自然历史博物馆古人类研究所合作，以直立人中的"爪哇人"和"北京人"为参照，用计算机对挤压变形的头骨加以校正、修复，成功地复原出Ⅱ号头骨化石的计算机三维模型。测定其脑容量值为1065毫升，接近"北京人"的平均值1075毫升，证明"郧县人"可能处于比较原始的直立人阶段。

3

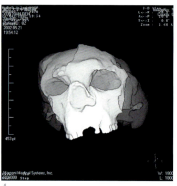

4

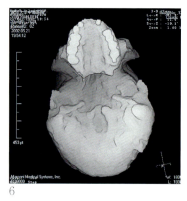

5

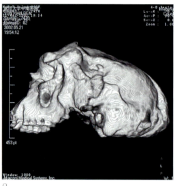

6

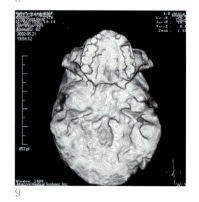

7

8

9

郧县人Ⅱ号头骨化石CT扫描
CT scanning of Yunxian Man Cranjum II
1.头骨矢状位→2.冠状位→3.头骨多平面二维重建→4-6.头骨表面遮盖重建→7-9.头骨三维重建的容积重建

法国电脑工程师在Intel 研究所进行郧县人II号头骨的计算机三维模型复原
French computer engineer doing computer-aided 3D reconstruction of Yunxian Man Cranium II at Intel Research Center

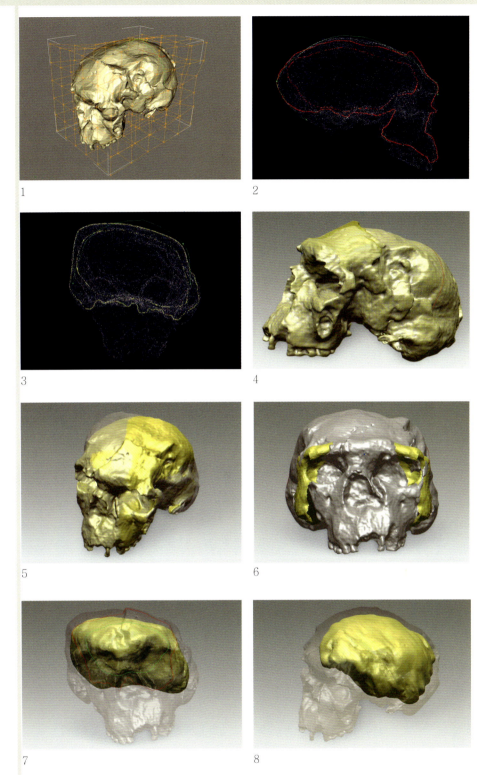

1　2

3　4

5　6

7　8

郧县人II号头骨计算机三维复原和铸模
3D reconstrunction and molding of Yunxian Man Cranium II

1.模型的三维定位→2.正中矢状位轮廓图比较→3.冠状位轮廓比较→4.额骨复位→5.顶骨矫形→6.颧弓和眉脊修复→7.头骨脑内模三维造像（正面）→8.头骨脑内模三维造像（侧面）→9.头骨的复原轨迹→10.经计算机校正后的郧县人II号头骨铸模

郧县人II号头骨化石复原以北京人XII号头骨颅冠状弧和爪哇人Sangiran 17号头骨颅矢状弧作为主要的参考对象，以控制头骨复原的颅顶弧度。

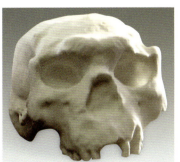

9　10

我们从何处来？

我们身上有这么多复杂的因素，显示我们是人类进化中的一个重要环节。我们像猿而又像人，我们从何而来？研究发现，我们的脑容量在1000毫升以上，臼齿粗硕，与南方古猿的牙齿相似，古人类学家认为我们的祖先是南方古猿和能人。

Where Did We Come from?

The presence of so many complicated features about us indicates our importance in the evolution of mankind. Where did we, who resembled both ape and man, come from? Researchers have found that we had a brain volume of over 1,000 ml, and thick, sturdy cheek teeth like those of *Australopithecus*. Paleoanthropologists believe that we descended from *Australopithecus* and *Homo habilis*.

"从南方古猿到人"   From *Australopithecus* to Man

人类起源于古猿。由于环境的变化，古猿从树栖生活到地面生活。四肢发生分化，开始直立行走，前肢可以使用天然工具，逐渐学会制造工具，完成了从猿到人的进化历程。在劳动和生活中产生了语言。距今1400万－800万年的腊玛古猿可能是从猿到人早期的代表，距今400万年的南方古猿可能是晚期的代表。目前一般认为，古猿转变为人类始祖的时间约在700万年前，人类进化约有四个阶段：

(1) 南方古猿（约440万－150万年）。南方古猿是最早的人科成员，它与猿类最为重要的区别是能够直立行走。

(2) 能人（约250万－160万年）。能人是最早的人属成员。能人脑容量平均637毫升，明显比南方古猿扩大，能制造简单的工具。肯尼亚发现的1470号人是其代表。

(3) 直立人（约150万－20万年，旧称猿人）。他们的脑容量在1000毫升左右，能制造先进的石器，有了简单分工，会使用火。印度尼西亚的爪哇人，我国的元谋人、蓝田人、郧县人、北京人等都属于直立人。

(4) 智人（约20万年至今）。智人生活在更新世的中、晚期，早期智人距今20万－5万年。他们接近现代人，能制作式样不同的石器，甚至有宗教意识。欧洲的尼安德特人，我国的金牛山人、大荔人、丁村人、长阳人、马坝人等，都属于早期智人。晚期智人是生活在更新世晚期后段（约5万年前）直到今天的人类。欧洲的克罗马农人和我国的山顶洞人、柳江人、资阳人等属于晚期智人。他们除了工具原始外已和现代人相似，保留了很少的原始性状，如头骨壁较厚。他们已有原始的艺术、宗教和社会组织。从生物学角度看，现代全世界各色人种属于同一个智人种。

Man evolved from paleolithic ape. Because of environmental changes, arboreal paleolithic ape came to live on the ground. Their limbs started to have different functions. They began to walk upright, and with their forelimbs they began to use natural tools and gradually learned to make tools. Thus they completed the evolution from ape to man. They developed language in their work and life. *Ramapithecus* living 14 million to 8 million years ago may be typical of the early stage of the evolution, while *Australopithecus* living 4 million years ago may be typical of its late stage. The general view is that paleolithic ape became the early man some 7 million years ago. The evolution of man experienced four stages:

(1) *Australopithecus* (approximately 4.4million-1.5million years ago), the earliest Hominidae, differed from pongidae mainly in the ability to walk upright.

(2) *Homo habilis* (approximately 2.5million-1.6million years ago), the earliest *Homo*, had an average brain volume of 637 ml, considerably larger than that of *Australopithecus*; was able to make simple tools. Typical species: '1470 Man' discovered in Kenya.

(3) *Homo erectus* (approximately from 1.5 million to 200,000 years ago, formerly known as 'ape-man'), had a brain volume of about 1,000 ml; was able to make advanced stone tools and use fire; had simple division of labor. Species discovered: Java Man in Indonesia, and Yuanmou Man, Lantian Man, Yunxian Man, and Peking Man in China.

(4) *Homo sapiens* (approximately 200,000 years ago to now) lived in middle and late Pleistocene. Early *Homo sapiens* lived 200,000-50,000 years ago. They closely resembled modern man and were able to make different kinds of stone tools; they even had religious consciousness. Species discovered include *H.S.neanderthalensis* in Europe and Jinniushan Man, Dali Man, Dingcun Man, Changyang Man and Maba Man in China. Late *Homo sapiens* refers to mankind existing from the last stage of late Pleistocene (approximately 50,000 years ago) till the present day. Discovered species include Cro-Magnon Man in Europe and Upper Cave Man, Liujiang Man, and Ziyang Man in China. Except for their primitive tools, they resembled modern man and retained few primitive physical features, such as thick skulls. They had primitive arts, religions and social organizations. In biological terms, peoples of different skin colors in the modern world belong to the same *Homo sapiens* species.

撒海尔人乍得种（托
麦人）也许就是人们
一直在寻找的、具有
人和猿混合特征的人
猿最近的共同祖先

Last common ancestor
it should have a mosaic
of features reminiscent of
both apes and humans—
but that's true of several
species already found, so
identification might be
tough

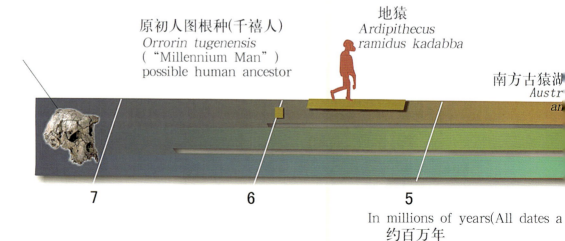

原初人图根种(千禧人)
Orrorin tugenensis
（"Millennium Man"）
possible human ancestor

地猿
Ardipithecus
ramidus kadabba

南方古猿湖
Austr
an

7　　　　　　　　6　　　　　　　5

In millions of years(All dates a
约百万年

人类进化图

Human family tree

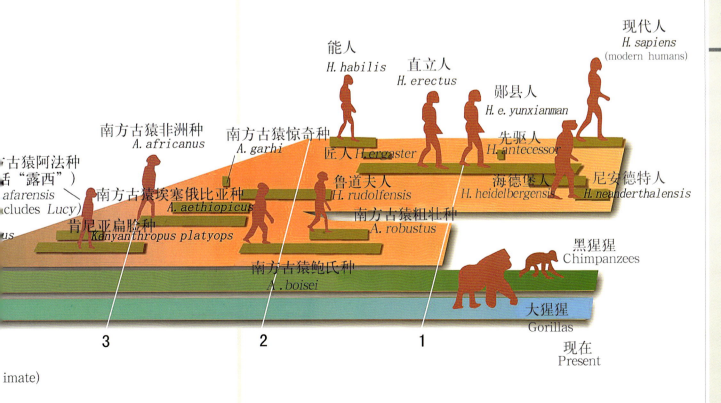

现代人
H. sapiens
(modern humans)

能人
H. habilis

直立人
H. erectus

郧县人
H. e. yunxianman

先驱人
H. antecessor

南方古猿非洲种
A. africanus

南方古猿惊奇种
A. garhi

匠人 *H. ergaster*

南方古猿阿法种
舌 "露西"）
afarensis
cludes *Lucy*)

南方古猿埃塞俄比亚种
A. aethiopicus

鲁道夫人
H. rudolfensis

海德堡人
H. heidelbergensis

尼安德特人
H. neanderthalensis

us

肯尼亚扁脸种
Kenyanthropus platyops

南方古猿粗壮种
A. robustus

黑猩猩
Chimpanzees

南方古猿鲍氏种
A. boisei

大猩猩
Gorillas

3

2

1

现在
Present

imate)

现代人在自然界中的位置简表
Modern man's place in nature

界 Kingdom 动物界（Animalia）

门 Phylum 脊椎动物门（Chordata）

亚门 Subphylum 脊椎动物亚门（Vertebrata）

纲 Class 哺乳纲（Mammalia）

目 Order 灵长目（Primates）

科 Family 人科（Hominidae）

属 Genus 人属（*Hominidae*）

种 Species 智人种（*Homo sapiens*）

南方古猿生活场景
Life of *Australopithecus*

南方古猿 *Australopithecus*

南方古猿属于灵长目人科，生活在距今400万－150万年。1924年首先发现于非洲南部的汤恩（Taungs）。研究者命名有南方古猿始祖种、南方古猿湖畔种、南方古猿阿法种、南方古猿非洲种、南方古猿惊奇种、南方古猿粗壮种、南方古猿鲍氏种、南方古猿埃塞俄比亚种等8个。南方古猿非洲种身高1.2米左右，脑容量440－500毫升，已能直立行走和使用工具。南方古猿演化出早期人类——人属。人科与猿科的惟一区别是直立行走。

南方古猿分粗壮和纤细两个类型，分别身高约1.5、1.2 米。粗壮型颅骨有明显的矢状脊，面骨相对较大，门齿、犬齿较小，以植物性食物为主，距今150万年前就灭绝；南方古猿阿法种和非洲种属纤细型，颅骨比较光滑，面骨比较小，杂食。纤细型进一步演化成了能人。南方古猿在名称上虽然叫古猿，学者们已认为它是人科的早期成员，也是我们郧县人的始祖。

Australopithecus, a family of primates, existed 4 million-1.5 million years ago. It was first discovered in Taungs in the south of Africa in 1924. Eight types have been identified: *A. ramidus*, *A. anamensis*, *A. afarensis*, *A. africanus*, *A. garhi*, *A. robustus*, *A. boisei*, and *A. aethiopicus* according to different materials. *A. africanus* stood about 1.2 meters tall, with a brain volume of 440-500 ml and the ability to walk and use tools. *Australopithecus* evolved into the early man—*Homo*. Hominidae differs from pongidae only in the ability to walk upright.

Australopithecus is divided into two types: the robust and the slender, the former measuring about 1.5 m tall and the latter 1.2 m. *A. robustus* has a prominent sagittal ridge, relatively large facial bones, and small incisors and canines; it was predominantly herbivore, and its extinction occurred 1.5 million years ago. *A. afarensis* and *A. africanus* were of the slender type. They had smooth skulls and relatively small facial bones, and it was omnivorous. The slender type evolved into *Homo habilis*. Scholars believe that *Australopithecus* was an early species of Hominidae, and the primogenitor of Yunxian Man.

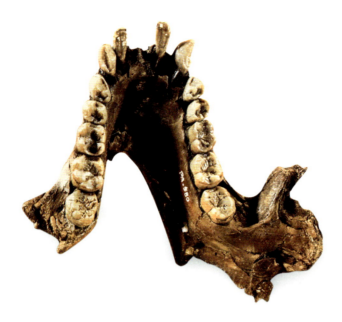

禄丰腊玛古猿下颌骨化石
Fossil of inferior maxilla of *Ramapithecus lufengensis*

腊玛古猿是从猿演化到人的过渡类型。1976年在云南禄丰石灰坝的褐煤层中发现了距今约800万年的一个古猿类型的下颌骨和1000多枚牙齿化石，下颌骨齿弓则呈规则的拱型，与早期直立人相似。命名为"禄丰西瓦古猿"（*Sivapithecus lufengensis*）。

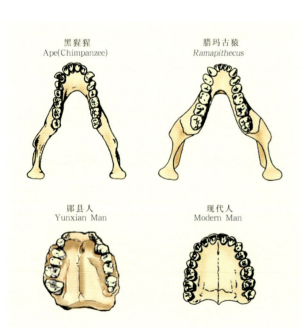

黑猩猩
Ape(Chimpanzee)

腊玛古猿
Ramapithecus

郧县人
Yunxian Man

现代人
Modern Man

古猿与人类口腔的比较图

Comparison on mouth between ape and man

大猩猩、南方古猿、能人、直立人、智人颅骨及脑容量比较图
Comparison on cranium and brain volume between gorilla, *Australopithecus*, *Homo habilis*, *Homo erectus* and *Homo sapiens*

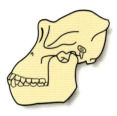

大猩猩(420ml)
Gorilla

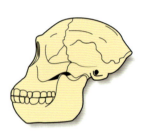

南方古猿(440 – 500ml)
Australopithecus

能人(640ml)
Homo habills

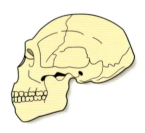

直立人(1000ml)
Homo erectus

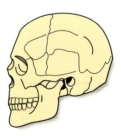

智人(1500ml)
Homo sapiens

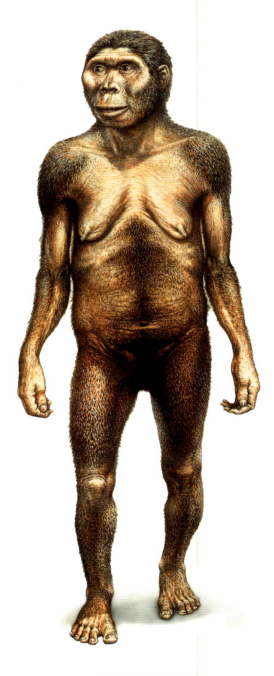

南方古猿阿法种复原图
Reconstruction drawing of *A. afarensis*

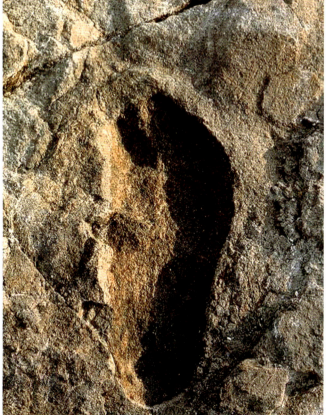

1978年，玛丽·利基在奥杜威峡谷发现了350万年南方古猿阿法种留下的脚印
Fossilized *A. afarensis* footprints dating from 3.5 million years ago were discovered by Mary Leaky at Olduvai Gorge in 1978.

约翰逊 和 "露西"
D. Johanson and "Lucy"
1974年约翰逊在埃塞俄比亚的哈达发现距今350万年的南方古猿阿法种"露西"，能直立行走，被认为是现代人类的祖先。

乍得人头骨化石
Toumai Cranium

2001年发现距今约700万年的乍得人"杜马伊"（土语的意思为"旱季前出生的孩子"，即"生活希望"），它能直立行走，是迄今发现的最早人种化石。

爱蒙德·达特(1893–1988)
Raymond Dart (1893–1988)

汤恩头骨化石
Cranium discovered at Taungs

1924年爱蒙德·达特在南非开普省的汤恩采石场首次发现的南方古猿幼儿的头骨。它头骨很像猿，脑容量虽小，但是它比黑猩猩的脑更像人；牙齿与人类牙齿相近。重要的是其枕骨大孔与人类相同位于颅底，表明已能直立行走。他于是提出汤恩是位于猿和人之间的类型，并定名为南方古猿非洲种。此前，多数科学家认为发达的大脑才是人的标志。

南方古猿非洲种头骨化石(Sts5)

Cranium fossil *of A. africanus*(Sts5)

1947年，罗伯特·布鲁姆在南非发现了一个保存完好的成年女性头骨（今天认为是男性），命名为"Ples"。距今250万年，脑容量为485毫升。它的发现表明南方古猿已能直立行走和奔跑，解决了汤恩小孩是否为人科的争论。

罗伯特·布鲁姆（1866－1951）
Robert Broom（1866－1951）

南方古猿粗壮种头骨化石

Cranium fossil of *A. robustus*

1938年，在南非约翰内斯堡以北的克罗姆德莱（Kromdraai）发现了南方古猿化石，有头骨片、颌骨、牙齿、臂骨、手骨和足骨等，明显比南方古猿非洲种粗壮。骨骼接近猿而不是人，布鲁姆把它定名为傍人（意为类似于人）粗壮种。后被命名为南方古猿粗壮种。

能人 *Homo Habilis*

"能人"的意思是手巧的人，是能制造工具的人，属人科，人属，能人种，生活在250万－200万年前。1961年乔纳森·利基领导的考查队在奥杜威峡谷发现了"能人"成年人的头骨化石。头骨壁相对较薄，推测其脑容量达到800毫升。身体比南方古猿轻巧，已能制造工具，代表了现代人的这一支的早期人类类型。1964年，达特建议命名它为能人，作为人属的早期成员。

Homo habilis means man skillful enough to make tools. It belongs to the species of *Homo habilis*, the genus of *Hominidae*, and the family of Hominidae. It existed 2.5million-2 million years ago. The cranium fossil of an adult *Homo habilis* was discovered by a team led by Jonathan Leakey at Olduvai Gorge in 1961. The skull is relatively thin, and its brain volume is estimated to be 800 ml. With a body more slender and agile than that of *Australopithecus* and the ability to make tools, it represents the early type of modern man. In 1964, at the suggestion of Dart, it was named *Homo habilis*, as an early member of *Hominidae*.

能人制作石器图
Homo habilis making stone tools

理查德·利基（1944－）
Richard E. Leakey（1944－）

1470号人头骨化石
Cranium of 1470 Man

1972年理查德·利基在肯尼亚卢多尔夫湖东岸发现距今约190万年的KNM-ER1470号头骨（KNM是肯尼亚国立博物馆的缩写，ER是东卢多夫的缩写），脑容量约775毫升，没有明显突出的眉脊，肢骨也和现代人相似。1470号头骨被认为属于能人类型。有学者因此认为智人是由能人直接演化而来，直立人不是人类的直系祖先。

直立人 *Homo Erectus*

直立人是人属的一个种，多数古人类学家认为是现代人类的祖先。这个种在更新世早、中期都有化石发现，是旧石器时代早期的人类。直立人的平均脑容量比能人大，约为智人的74%，前额后倾，牙齿的体积亦较小，它比能人更接近现代人，平均身高约160厘米。直立人制作和使用的工具比能人明显进步。

Homo erectus is a species of *Hominidae*. Most paleoanthropologists believe it to be the ancestor of modern man. Fossil remains of the species date from the early and middle Pleistocene. It was a hominid of the early Paleolithic Age. It had a larger brain volume (about 74% of that of *Homo sapiens*) than *Homo habilis*. With a reclining forehead, relatively small teeth and an average height of 160 cm, it bore a closer resemblance to modern man than *Homo habilis*. It could make and use remarkably better tools than *Homo habilis*.

元谋人牙齿化石
Tooth fossils of Yuanmou Man

1965年在云南元谋发现中国最早的直立人牙齿化石，其时代略与魁人相当。

建始人牙齿化石
Tooth fossils of *Meganthropus paleojavanicus*

左：第三前臼齿：高2.9，长1，宽0.8cm
中：第一前臼齿：高1.9，长1.3，宽1.2cm
右：第三臼齿：高2.4，长1.3，宽1.1cm

1970年在建始县高坪龙骨山巨猿洞曾经发现巨猿牙齿100多个。伴生哺乳动物化石近100种，其地质时代为早更新世晚期。巨猿（*Gigantopithecus*）形体比人类大，下颌特征原始，距今约100万－10万年，目前仅在亚洲发现。

1998年，中国科学院启动了"早期人类起源及环境背景的研究"课题。鄂西山地是4个研究地点之一。1999－2000年，在建始巨猿洞进行了3次调查和发掘，又获得3枚"似人科成员的牙齿"。经专家鉴定，属于人科，人类的旁支魁人属（*Meganthropus*，亦认为是原始的直立人），古爪哇魁人种（*M. paleojavanicus*）。伴生哺乳动物化石87种。时代为早更新世。采用古地磁法的测年结果为距今215万－195万年。

建始巨猿洞洞内魁人牙齿化石发掘地点
Site where the tooth fossils of *Meganthropus* were unearthed

1999年建始巨猿洞出土的魁人伴生的动物化石

The animal fossils of *Meganthropus* discovered at Jianshi Juyuandong in 1999

中国黑熊下颌骨化石

Fossil of the inferior maxilla of *Ursus thibetanus*

长17.5、宽7cm

东方剑齿象牙齿化石

Teeth fossil of *Stegodon orientalis*

长12.5、宽8.5cm

大熊猫颌骨化石

Fossil of the jaw bone of *Ailuropoda melanoleuca*

长10.5、宽9cm

鹿角化石

Fossil of an antler

长22.5cm

乳齿象牙齿化石

Tooth fossil of *mastodon*

高5、长5、宽3.5cm

爪兽牙齿化石

Tooth fossils of *Chalicothere*

上：长3.1、宽2.4cm
下：长4.7、宽3.4cm

1999年建始巨猿洞出土的魁人使用的石器
Stone tools used by *Meganthropus* discovered at Jianshi Juyuandong in 1999

单直刃刮削器
Single-edged scraper
长3，宽2.6，厚1.5cm

有脊台面石片
Crested striking platforms
长30，宽27，厚11cm

多台面石核
Multi-platform core
长45，宽45，厚23cm

KNM—ER 3733非洲直立人头骨化石（或匠人）
Cranium KNM-ER 3733 *Homo erectus* (or *Homo ergaster*)

1975年由伯纳德·内格罗（Bernard Ngeneo）在肯尼亚北部发现的直立人头骨化石，年代约为200万年前。脑容量850毫升，头骨形态特征类似北京人。研究认为他已经有了语言的能力。

OH9 Reconstruction奥杜威峡谷9号头骨化石
OH9 Cranium from Olduvai Gorge

1960年由路易斯·利基(Louis leakey)发现于奥杜威峡谷的直立人，时代和郧县人相当，距今约120万年。

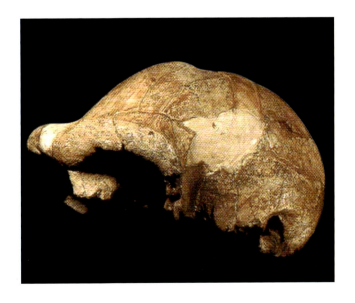

爪哇人头骨化石(Sangiran 17)
Cranium of Java Man (Sangiran 17)

1891年荷兰解剖学家杜布瓦在印度尼西亚爪哇岛的特里尼尔（Trinil）村附近，发现了一个不带脸面部分的头盖骨和一颗牙齿。次年又在同一地点发现了一根人的大腿骨。杜布瓦认为头骨脑容量940毫升，距今约70万年，这些化石属于人和猿之间的过渡种类，定名为"直立猿人"。

1969年，Towikromo在爪哇桑吉兰发现最完整的直立人（Sangiran 17），脑容量1000毫升，距今约80万年，最近认为其年代为距今约170万年。

第一个爪哇人的发现者杜布瓦（1858－1940）
Eugene Dubois (1858–1940), first discoverer of Java Man

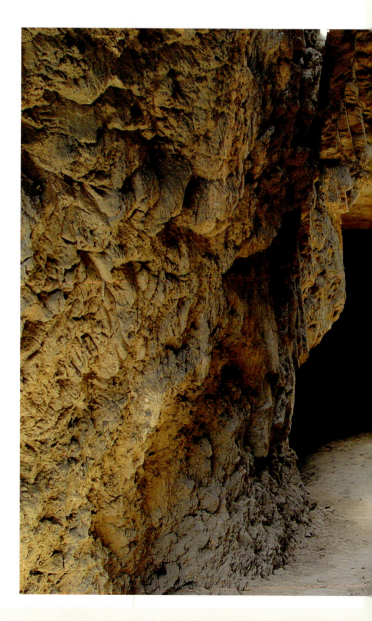

北京人头骨化石及其复原像
Cranium of Peking Man

高10.5，长17.7，宽14.2cm

旧石器时代早期，属直立人。1921年发现于北京房山县周口店龙骨山，以后经过多次发掘，发现5个头盖骨、头骨碎片、面骨、下颌骨、股骨等化石，其中在1929年发掘的第一个北京人的头盖骨化石在1941年遗失。1949年以后，又发掘出一件头盖骨和其他人骨化石，大体属于40个个体。北京人的头盖骨低平、额部后倾、眉脊粗壮，向前突出，面部较短，吻部前伸，牙齿比现代人粗大，说明它们保存有浓厚的原始形态。脑容量平均为1043毫升。北京人生活的年代为距今约50万年。

北京猿人复原像

郧县人 长江中游的远古人类

北京人化石出土地点之一——周口店
One of the sites at Zhoukoudian where fossils of Peking Man were unearthed

北京人生活场景
Life of Peking Man

发现第一个北京人头骨化石的裴文中（1904－1982）
Pei Wenzhong (1904–1982), discoverer of the first
Peking Man Cranium

贾兰坡在周口店遗址现场
Jia Lanpo, discoverer of the first Peking Man Cranium, at the site
（《周口店记事》，上海科学技术出版社，1999年）

步达生（1884－1934），加拿大古生物学家，曾
经任北京协和医院解剖科人类学教授，1926年他
命名北京周口店出土的牙齿化石为"中国猿人北京
种"。
Davidson Black (1884–1934), Canadian
paleoanthropologist. He initiated and supervised
the "Peking man" fieldwork at Zhoukoudian
and named the resulting *Homo erectus* fossils
"*Sinanthropus pekinensis*".

郧县梅铺直立人牙齿化石
Tooth fossils of *Homo erectus* from Meipu, Yun County

上：高0.8，齿面0.9×0.7cm
中：高2.2，齿面1.2×1.1cm
下：高1.5，齿面宽0.9cm

1975年在湖北省郧县梅铺龙骨洞中发现4枚牙齿化石，特征与北京人牙齿相似，属于直立人。伴生的动物化石有大熊猫、嵌齿象、桑氏缟鬣狗、中国貘、中国犀和小猪等20余种，代表的地质年代为早更新世，比北京人的动物群要早。

郧县梅铺龙骨洞远景和近景
Long-range and close view of Longgudong,
Meipu, Yun County

郧西白龙洞发掘现场
Site of the excavation of Bailongdong,
Yunxi

1976年在郧西县东15公里的白龙洞发现7枚直立人牙齿化石，其伴生动物群与北京人相当。

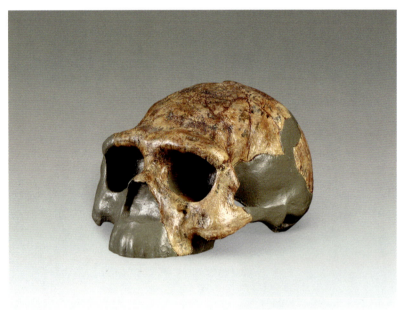

南京人头骨化石
Cranium of Nanjing Man

高11.4、长20.2、宽14.3cm

1993年在南京汤山发现2件晚期直立人头骨化石。据出土南京人化石特征和伴生的哺乳动物群，结合铀系法和电子自旋共振法测年研究，南京人距今约35万年。

蓝田人头骨化石
Cranium of Liantian Man

高12.1、长23.8、宽16.1cm

1964年在陕西蓝田县发现的公王岭古人类女性头骨化石。头盖骨低平，额部明显倾斜，眉脊骨粗壮，骨壁厚，吻部向前突出，表现出较为原始的形态。脑容量小，估计为780毫升。在蓝田人化石的层位中发现有大尖状器、砍砸器、刮削器和石球等石器。加工方法为简单的锤击法，石片一般未经第二步加工即付诸使用。共生的动物有41种，其中包括大熊猫、东方剑齿象、毛冠鹿，带有强烈的南方动物群的色彩。1965年在陈家窝发现老年女性的下颌骨化石。最新的研究结果，公王岭遗址距今约115万年，陈家窝地点距今约53万年。

郧县人 长江中游的远古人类

蓝田人遗址
Lantian Man site

我们向何处去？

南方古猿能直立行走，能人会制造工具。进化到直立人之后，我们的生存环境也有了变化，我们从森林来到原野，从山地来到平川，从非洲走向世界各地。我们的后代使用越来越复杂的石制工具，也学会了控制火；脑容量从南方古猿、能人的平均脑容量（分别是500、650毫升），逐渐增加到了1200毫升，成了有智慧的人类。随着人类繁衍和改造自然能力的增强，我们后代的天然食物来源也持续减少，他们发展为智人，进入到了农业革命的新石器时代。

Where Did We Go?

Australopithecus could walk upright and *Homo habilis* could make tools. When man evolved to the stage of *Homo erectus*, our living environment changed. We went out of forests to open fields, out of mountains to plains, and out of Africa to other parts of the world. Our descendants used increasingly complicated stone tools, and gained control of fire; their brain volume grew from the average of *Australopithecus* (500 ml) and *Homo habilis* (650 ml) to 1,200 ml, and they became intelligent humans. With the human population growing and their ability to change the nature increasing, our descendants experienced a steady decrease in natural food sources. They developed into *Homo sapiens*, and entered into the era of agriculture and the Neolithic Age.

智人 *Homo Sapiens*

智人是人类演化的最高阶段，它包括化石智人和现生智人。现生智人由直立人演化的化石智人进化而来。化石智人分早期和晚期，时间在距今20万－1万年间。早期智人化石在非洲、欧洲和亚洲都有发现，最早发现的是尼安德特人。中国较为重要的早期智人有陕西大荔人、辽宁金牛山人、四川马坝人、湖北长阳人等。晚期智人结构与现生人类基本一致。法国的克罗马农人是晚期智人最著名的代表。中国晚期智人化石已发现40余处，其中最重要的有湖北郧西人、广西柳江人、北京山顶洞人、贵州穿洞人、山西峙峪人等。

Homo sapiens is the highest stage of human evolution. It includes fossil *Homo sapiens* and modern *Homo sapiens*. Modern *Homo sapiens* evolved from fossil *Homo sapiens*, which in turn evolved from *Homo erectus*. Fossil *Homo sapiens* is divided into two types—the early and the late, and existed 200,000-10,000 years ago. Fossils of early *Homo sapiens* were discovered in Africa, Europe and Asia. The first *Homo sapiens* species discovered was the Neanderthal. Important early *Homo sapiens* species discovered in China are Dali Man in Shaanxi, Jinniushan Man in Liaoning, Maba Man in Sichuan, and Changyang Man in Hubei. Late *Homo sapiens* had roughly the same anatomy as modern man. Cro-Magnon Man found in France is the best known representative of late *Homo sapiens*. In China, more than 40 sites of late *Homo sapiens* fossils have been discovered. The most important species are Yunxi Man in Hubei, Liujiang Man in Guangxi, Upper Cave Man in Beijing, Chuandong Man in Guizhou and Shiyu Man in Shanxi.

阿拉戈人XXI头骨化石
Arago Man XXI Cranium

高23.4，长13.5，宽15.1cm

1971年发现于法国西南部的阿拉戈（Arago），距今约40万年，混合了直立人和早期智人的特点。

尼安德特人复原图
Reconstruction drawing of a Neanderthal

尼安德特人头骨化石
Neanderthal Cranium

高14，长23.6，宽15.9cm

尼安德特人1856年发现于德国杜塞尔多夫附近尼安德特河谷的一个小洞内，属于早期智人阶段。广义上它代表一个人群，主要分布于西欧，包括比利时、法国、德国、意大利。生存时代为晚更新世，著名的莫斯特文化就是他们创造的。尼安德特人的头盖骨低平，眉脊粗大，脑容量为1230毫升。在法国还发现一具完整的尼安德特人，尸体旁放有燧石、石英块以及野牛与驯鹿的骨架，说明尼安德特人时代已有埋葬。

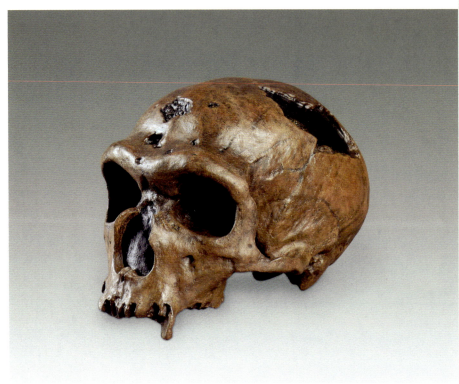

尼安德特人埋葬死者
A buried Neanderthal

佩特拉洛纳人头骨化石
Petralona Cranium

除了尼安德特人之外，欧洲还发现了同时有晚期直立人和早期智人特点的化石。1960年在希腊卡尔基迪省（Khalkidiki）的佩特拉洛纳发现的早期智人就是如此，其脑容量1220毫升，面颅较宽，距今约50万－25万年。

丁村人牙齿化石
Dingcun Man tooth fossils

左：长1.4，宽0.5cm
中：长1.9，宽0.7cm
右：长1.1，宽0.8cm

1953年发现于山西襄汾丁村。距今约12万年。

昂栋人头骨化石
Ngandong Man Cranium

1931－1941年期间，在印度尼西亚爪哇岛梭罗河沿岸的昂栋村附近，陆续发现了距今约20万年、具有直立人和智人特征的多个头骨化石，平均脑容量1154毫升。这批化石材料被定名为梭罗智人（*Homo sapiens soloenisis*），亦称为昂栋人或者梭罗人。时代属晚更新世。昂栋人多年来一直存在分类问题，有人认为应归属于直立人；也有学者认为应属于早期智人。

马坝人头骨化石
Maba Man Cranium

高9.5, 长19.4, 宽14cm

1958年发现于广东曲江县马坝狮子山。头盖骨的骨壁较薄, 脑颅明显隆起, 高度大于北京人, 脑容量也较大。分类上归入早期智人, 距今约20万—10万年。

马坝人头骨化石复原
Reconstruction of Maba Man Cranium

长阳人化石发现地点
Site where Changyang Man
fossils were discovered

麝上颌骨化石
Maxilla fossil of *Moschidae*

1995年鲢鱼山遗址出土
长 7. 宽5cm

长阳人牙齿化石
Changyang Man tooth fossil

1956、1957年在湖北长阳县下钟家湾的龙洞内发现早期智人的上颌骨和一枚臼齿化石。这是湖北首次发现古人类化石。从上颌骨化石标本上可以看见，犬齿发达，鼻腔底壁不如现代人那样凹；颌的倾斜度与现代人接近，比北京人进步。伴生出土的动物化石有大熊猫、东方剑齿象、中国犀等，时代为晚更新世早期。距今约20万－10万年。

鹿下牙床化石
Teethridge fossils of *Cerviae*

1995年鲢鱼山遗址出土
左：长 9.1. 宽3.5cm
右：长6.8. 宽3.5cm

中国貘牙齿化石

Tooth fossil of *Tapirus sinensis*

1995年鲢鱼山遗址出土
长4，宽3cm

梅氏犀右上颌骨化石

Maxilla fossil of *Rhinoceros mercki* Kaup

长阳伴峡小洞出土
长24，宽15cm

犀牛下颌骨化石

Inferior maxilla fossil of *Rhinocerotidae sinensis*

1995年鲢鱼山遗址出土
长26，宽15cm

苏门羚头骨化石

Capricornis sumatraensis fossil

1995年鲢鱼山遗址出土
长23，宽12cm

郧西黄龙洞外景
View of Huanglongdong in Yunxi

郧西人牙齿化石
Yunxi Man tooth fossils

上左：下颌右第二臼齿：高0.6，长1.6，宽1.2cm
上中：下颌左第二门齿：高0.6，长1.5，宽1.1cm
上右：上颌左犬齿：高0.8，长1.5，宽1cm
下左：下颌左第三臼齿：高0.7，长1.6，宽1.1cm
下右：上颌左第三臼齿：高0.7，长1.3，宽1.2cm

2004年6月至8月中旬，湖北省文物考古研究所在对郧西黄龙洞的抢救性发掘中，相继发现距今约10万年的5枚古人类牙齿化石和一批重要的伴生动物群化石。化石石化程度较轻，特征与晚期人类比较接近，是目前东亚发现最早的晚期智人。

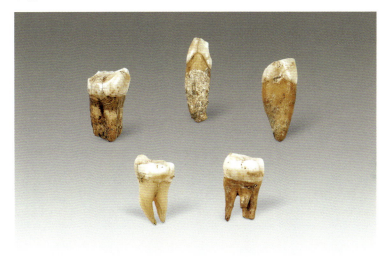

黄龙洞洞内清理并发现智人类牙齿化石
Discovery of *Homo sapiens* tooth fossils in Huanglongdong

郧西人伴生的动物化石
Fossils of animals sharing the habitat of Yunxi Man

郧西人伴生动物的化石至少有50种，其中翼手目类化石、裸腹重唇鱼化石等都是国内首次发现。

The fossils belong to at least 50 species. Among them, fossils of *Chiroptera* and *Diptychus kaznakovi* were first discovered in China.

藏鼠兔下颌骨化石
Inferior maxilla fossils of *Ochotona thibetana*

左：2.3×1.8×1.5cm
右：1.1×1×1.3cm

翼手目类下颌骨化石
Inferior maxilla fossils of *Chiroptera* species

上左：印度假吸血蝠 *Megaderm lyra*，0.8×0.5×0.3cm
上右：大马蹄蝠 *Hipposideros armiger*，0.9×0.5×0.4cm
下左：斑蝠 *Scotomanes emarginatus*，0.8×0.5×0.4cm
下右：马铁菊头蝠 *Rhinolophus ferrumequinum*，0.9×0.7×0.3cm

裸複重唇鱼下咽齿化石
Tooth fossils of *Diptychus kaznakovi*

左：0.9×0.7×0.6cm
右：1.1×1×0.5cm

啮齿目下颌骨化石
Inferior maxilla fossils of Rodentia species

左：赤腹松鼠左下颌骨 *Callosciurus erythraeus*，1.9×1.2×0.5cm
中：赤腹松鼠右下颌骨 *Callosciurus erythraeus*，2.2×1.3×1.5cm
右：侧纹岩松鼠右下颌骨 *Sciurotamias forresti*，1.3×2.1×0.7cm

白腹管鼻蝠头骨化石
Cranium of *Murina leucogaster*
上：1.1×1×0.5cm
下：0.8×0.5×0.3cm

华南虎牙齿化石
Tooth fossils of *Panthera tigris amoyensis*
左：1.8×1.2×0.5cm
右：2.1×1.5×0.5cm

华南豪猪下颌骨化石
Inferior maxilla fossil of *Hystrix subcristata*
2.8×1.5×1.2cm

基氏贝尔格犀牙齿化石
Lower tooth fossil (left) and upper tooth fossil (right) of *Dicerorhinus kirchbergensis*
左：下牙 3.8×2.6×2.2cm
右：上牙 3.1×2.2×1.5cm

东方剑齿象牙齿化石
Deciduous molar fossils (left) and molar fossil (right) of *Stegodon orientalis*
左：乳臼齿 5.5×4.1×2.6cm
右：臼齿 5.1×3.2×2.5cm

克罗马农人头骨化石
Cro-Magnon Man Cranium

高14.7，长20.1，宽13.9cm

1868年法国地质学家在法国多尔多涅省埃西德塔雅克附近克罗马农进行发掘，发现了最完整的史前人类文明，这些史前人类被命名为克罗马农人。克罗马农人的体质与现在人几乎没有区别，是生物学意义上的现代人，距今在4万－1万年之间。他们在工具制作、艺术创作方面都超过了尼安德特人，欧洲最早的壁画、艺术雕刻、乐器都是他们的作品。

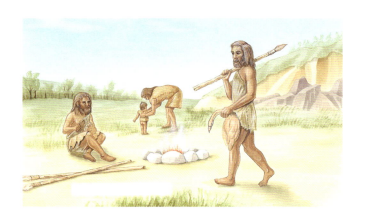

克罗马农人营地
Camp of Cro–Magnon Man

柳江人头骨化石
Cranium of Liujiang Man

高14.4，长20.6，宽14.3cm

1958年在广西柳江县通天岩发现距今约4万年的晚期智人类。化石人种为蒙古人种，形态具有一定的原始性，也带有热带地区人类的共同特征，如鼻骨宽阔，身材较为矮小，与现代的东南亚人接近。在郧西人牙齿化石发现之前，一般认为柳江人是中国发现最早的晚期智人化石。

山顶洞人头骨化石
Crania of Upper Cave Man

上左：高14.9，长22，宽14cm
上右：高15.6，长21.7，宽13.8cm
下：高14.7，长20.2，宽13.9cm

1930年在北京房山县周口店龙骨山发现了3件头骨化石，共8个个体，既有婴儿，也有少年和60岁以上的老人。体质特征已接近现代人，脑容量也达到1300－1500毫升，与现代人相一致，属晚期智人。同时发现一些文化遗物，石器有砍砸器，加工方法与北京人相同。发现的骨针是我国最早发现的旧石器时代缝纫工具。骨针的钻孔技术已相当先进。山顶洞人已有墓葬。在三具完整的人头骨和一些躯干骨周围，发现有散布的赤铁矿粉末和一些随葬品，表明山顶洞人已经有了审美意识和宗教信仰。时代为旧石器时代晚期，距今约1.8万年。

山顶洞人的生活场景
Life of Upper Cave Man

山顶洞人的装饰品
Ornaments of Upper Cave Man

郧县人 长江中游的远古人类

汉阳人头骨化石
Hanyang Man Cranium

高11，长18，宽13cm

1997年，毛凑元在武汉汉南区纱帽镇长江江滩采集一件头骨化石，属25－35岁的女性个体，形态特征与四川资阳人相似，属晚期智人类型。汉南区原为汉阳县，定名为"汉阳人"。发现化石的地点在纱帽山下游约300米处。考古调查发现了更新世堆积物并采集到1件砂岩石核。汉阳人头骨化石是否出于此层中，还有待今后做工作。

汉阳纱帽山
Shamaoshan of Hanyang

旧石器时代的技术 Paleolithic Technology

旧石器时代人类制造石器的技术可分为五个阶段。第一阶段以石核制品（如砍砸器）为特征，它发源于非洲，并且随着直立人的扩散而传播到欧洲与亚洲。第二阶段约在150万年前，又称阿舍利工业，它以大型两面器，特别是手斧为特征。第三阶段约出现在15万年前，又称旧石器时代中期技术，或莫斯特工业，以制作细小的尖状器和刮削器的石核修整技术为特征。第四阶段以石叶为特征的旧石器时代晚期技术出现在3.5万年前。以细石器为特征的第五阶段出现在2万－1万年前。但是亚洲的石器文化一直以砍砸器为主，没有明显的阶段划分。

Technology in the Paleolithic Age can be divided into five stages. The first stage was characterized by stone core artifacts (such as choppers); it originated in Africa, and was brought by *Homo erectus* to Europe and Asia. The second stage, dating from about 1.5 million years ago, is named Acheulean industry; it was characterized by large bifaces, especially adaes. The third stage, starting from about 150,000 years ago, is known as mid-Paleolithic technology, or Mousterian industry; it was characterized by the making of tiny pointed tools and scrapers as well as the trimming of cores. The fourth stage, or late Paleolithic technology, appeared 35,000 years ago; it was characterized by the stone blade. The fifth stage, characterized by microliths, appeared 20,000-10,000 years ago. However, Asian stone tool culture cannot be divided into distinct stages, because choppers were always predominant.

北京人的盘状砍砸器
Circular choppers used by Peking Man

蓝田人的尖状器
Points used by Lantian Man

丁村人的多边形器
Polygonal tool used by Dingcun Man

丁村人的尖状器
Points used by Dingcun Man

1971年大冶石龙头出土石器
Stone tools from Shilongtou, Daye in 1971

最大：石核，长12.5、宽9.3cm
最小：石片，长5.5、宽3.2cm

1999年长阳伴峡小洞出土石砍砸器
Stone choppers unearthed at Xiaodong,
Banxia, Changyang in 1999

左：长8、宽8.5、厚2.5cm
右：长11.6、宽6.5、厚3cm

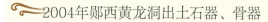

2004年郧西黄龙洞出土石器、骨器
Stone and bone tools unearthed at Huanglongdong, Yunxi 2004

石锥
Stone drill

5.5×3.5×1.5cm

石砍砸器
Stone chopper

11×7×2cm

骨器化石
Bone tool fossils

骨铲：10×2.2×1cm
骨尖状器：8×5×1cm

石刮削器
Stone scraper

3.1×2×0.7cm

骨片化石
Sclerite fossil

4.2×2.2×0.7cm

锤击石片
Stone flake

4.7×3.8×1.5cm

石手镐
Stone hand axe

11×10×5cm

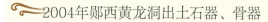

长江中游文明之旅
A Journey to Mid-Yangtze River Civilization

1968年房县樟脑洞出土石器
Stone tools unearthed at Zhangnaodong, Fang County in 1968

石尖状器
Stone points

上：长6.5，宽3.7cm
中左：长6.8，宽4cm
中右：长8.5，宽5.5cm
下：长8，宽7cm

石核
Stone core

长9.5，宽9，厚7cm

房县樟脑洞外景
View of Zhangnaodong in Fang County

1992年江陵鸡公山出土旧石器时代晚期石器
Stone tools of Paledolithic Age unearthed at Jigongshan,
Jiangling in 1992

尖状器
Points
左：长16.5、宽10.5、厚6cm
右：长16.7、宽10.5、厚6cm

刮削器
Scrapers
左：刮削器：长5.1、宽4.7、厚2.5cm
右：凹缺刮削器：长6.7、宽4.5、厚2.5cm

砍砸器
Chopper
长10.2、宽9.4、厚5cm

江陵鸡公山旧石器时代晚期遗址发掘现场
Site of the excavation of the late Paleolithic site on
Jigongshan, Jiangling

石器制造示意图

Making of a stone tool

旧石器时代的石器制造方法分为直接打击法和间接打击法。直接打击法有以下几种：(1)锤击法：以石锤直接在石料上进行打击的；(2)碰砧法：将所选石料往另一更大的石砧上碰击，直到手中石料合乎需要；(3)砸击法：将所选石料的一端置于石砧上，以石锤打击另一端。间接打击法是石锤不直接落在石料上，而是通过木棒等中介物的传导，见于旧石器时代晚期。

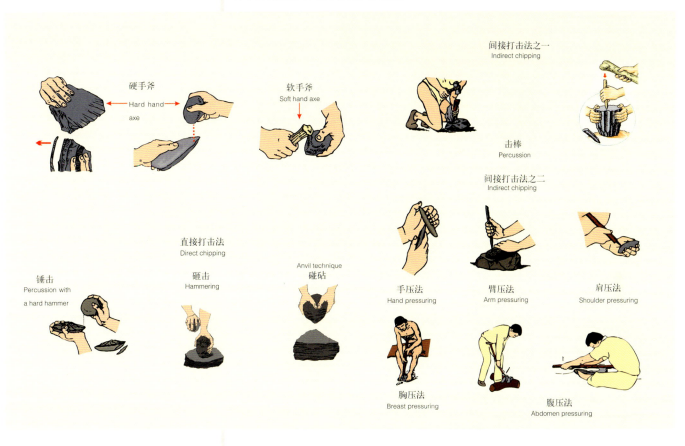

硬手斧
Hard hand axe

软手斧
Soft hand axe

间接打击法之一
Indirect chipping

击棒
Percussion

间接打击法之二
Indirect chipping

直接打击法
Direct chipping

手压法
Hand pressuring

臂压法
Arm pressuring

肩压法
Shoulder pressuring

锤击
Percussion with a hard hammer

砸击
Hammering

Anvil technique
碰砧

胸压法
Breast pressuring

腹压法
Abdomen pressuring

石器类型图

Types of stone tools

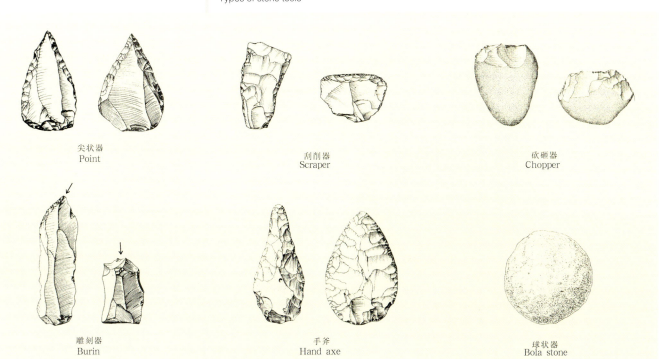

尖状器
Point

刮削器
Scraper

砍砸器
Chopper

雕刻器
Burin

手斧
Hand axe

球状器
Bola stone

郧西人时代的植物化石
Plant fossil dating from the age of Yunxi Man

人类使用火
Using Fire

使用火是人类利用自然的一次飞跃。周口店北京人遗址首次发现人类的用火痕迹。2004年在以色列Gesher Benot Ya'aqov遗址又发现了距今79万年的人类用火来制造工具、加工食物的证据。1999年在湖北长阳伴峡和鲢鱼山分别发现距今13万年和12万年左右的古人类用火痕迹，这在长江中游还是首次发现。2004年又在郧西黄龙洞发现郧西人的用火灰烬。

Using fire represents a great leap forward to explore and utilize the Nature. The earliest traces of using fire were discovered in Peking Man site at Zhoukoudian. In 2004, evidences for making tools and cooking by fire were unearthed at Gesher Benot Ya'aqov site dating from 790,000 years ago in Israel. In 1999, traces of using fire were found at Banxia and Lianyushan in Changyang, Hubei Province, with the two respectively dating back to 130,000 and 120,000 years ago. This is the first of such traces in the middle reaches of the Yangtze. The year of 2004 also witnessed the great discovery of the ashes left by Yunxi Man in Huanglongdong, Yunxi.

郧西人用火灰烬
Cinder left by Yunxi Man

长阳伴峡小洞人类用火痕迹
Traces of using fire left by humans at Xiaodong, Banxia, Changyang
1999年在长阳伴峡发现距今13万年左右的古人类用火痕迹，这是目前长江中游的首次发现。

长阳伴峡小洞旧石器遗址发掘现场
Site of Paleolithic Age at Xiaodong, Banxia, Changyang

以色列Gesher Benot Ya'aqov遗址发现距今79万年的人类用火痕迹
Evidence of using fire dating from 790,000 years ago discovered at Gesher Benot Ya'aqov site in Israel

人工取火图
Ways of getting fire

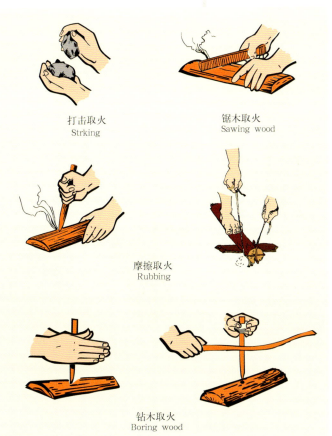

打击取火
Strking

锯木取火
Sawing wood

摩擦取火
Rubbing

钻木取火
Boring wood

现代智人的起源

The origin of modern *Homo sapiens*

自达尔文时代以来，依据化石形态的排序研究，现代智人是由多地区古人类进化而来。20世纪出现的细胞生物学和基因理论使现代智人多地区起源学说受到挑战，根据对女性线粒体的研究发现，全世界的现代人均源于约20万年前一位非洲女性，即"线粒体夏娃"；而对男性Y染色体的追踪也发现现代东亚人有非洲人特有的遗传标记。这对人类的多区进化论提出了挑战。

Since the age of Darwin, physical sequence study of fossils had indicated that modern *Homo sapiens* evolved from hominids in multiple regions. In the 20th century the multiregional theory was challenged by cytobiology and the gene theory. According to the gene theory, modern *Homo sapiens* spread from Africa to other parts of the world 200,000 years ago.

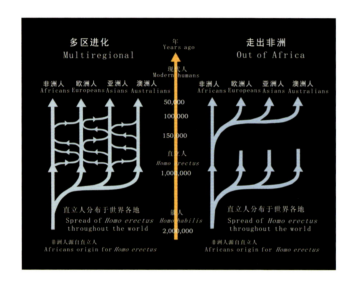

现代智人起源的简表
Diagrams of the origin of modern *Homo sapiens*
图左是"多地区假说"。直立人群体在接近200万年前从非洲向外扩张，定居于整个旧大陆。地区性群体之间的基因交流在整个旧大陆维持着遗传的连续性，在有直立人群体的地方普遍发生了向现代智人的进化。图右是"出非洲说"。现代智人在近期产生于非洲，很快扩张到旧大陆的其余部分，取代已存在那里的直立人和远古智人。

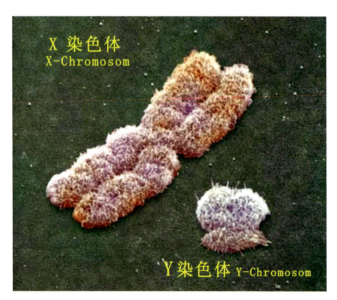

X和Y染色体
X and Y chromosome
细胞核内的Y染色体是遗传物质的载体。人的染色体有23对，即46条，其中22对叫"常染色体"，男性与女性的常染色体一样，余下的一对叫"性染色体"。男性的由一个X染色体和一个Y染色体组成（XY），女性的则由相同的X染色体组成（XX）。X染色体可以传子，也可以传女，而短小的Y染色体只能相传子，又被称为姓氏基因。

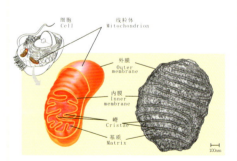

线粒体
Mitochondria
线粒体是真核细胞的重要细胞器，是动物细胞生成能量（ATP）的主要地点。线粒体的遗传基因（DNA）跟人的细胞核的DNA有质的不同，线粒体独立自主地复制繁衍，只能由母亲传递给女儿。因此其谱系树能够显示现代人类不同时期的基因突变，成为追踪现代人谱系来源的有效工具。

地 质 年 代 简 表 Geologic Chronological Table

宙 Eon	代 Era	纪 Period	世 Epoch	结束—开始（百万年）End – beginning (million years)	开始繁荣 Prosperity 植物 Flora	开始繁荣 Prosperity 动物 Fauna	
显生宙 Phanerozoic	新生代 Cenozoic	第四纪 Quaternary	全新世 Holocene	现代 Today – 0.01	被子植物 Angiosperm	人类 Homo	
			更新世 Pleistocene	0.01 – 1.8			
		第三纪 Tertiary	上新世 Pliocene	1.8 – 5.3		哺乳类 Mammalia	古猿出现 Ape
			中新世 Miocene	5.3 – 23			
			渐新世 Oligocene	23 – 36.5			
			始新世 Eocene	36.5 – 53			
			古新世 Palaeocene	53 – 65			灵长类出现 Primates
	中生代 Mesozoic	白垩纪 Cretaceous		65 – 145	裸子植物 Gymnosperm	爬行类 Reptile	鸟类出现Aves 恐龙繁殖 Dinosaurs
		侏罗纪 Jurassic		145 – 208			
		三叠纪 Triassic		208 – 248			恐龙、哺乳类出现 Dinosaurs，Mammalia
	古生代 Palaeozoic	二叠纪 Permian		248 – 290	蕨类 Pteridophyta 裸蕨 Psilopsid	两栖类 Amphibian	爬行类出现 两栖类繁殖 Amphibian，Reptiles
		石炭纪 Carboniferous		290 – 360			
		泥盆纪 Devonian		360 – 410		鱼类 Fishes	陆生无脊椎动物发展和两栖类出现 Invertebrate，Reptiles
		志留纪 Silurian		410 – 438			
		奥陶纪 Ordovician		438 – 510		无脊椎动物 Invertebrate	带壳动物爆发Shellfish erupted
		寒武纪 Cambrian		510 – 570			软体动物爆发Mollusk erupted
隐生宙 Cryptozoic	元古宙 Precambrian	震旦纪 Sinian 元古代 Proterozoic		570 – 800			
				800 – 2,500	高级藻类出现 Algae 海生藻类出现 Marine algae	低等无脊椎动物 Lower Invertebrate	
	太古宙 Archaean 太古代 Archaeozoic			2,500 – 3,875	真核藻类细菌与蓝菌（原始生命蛋白质出现）Eukaryotic Algae，Cyanophyta（Progenote）		
	冥古宙 Priscoan 冥古代 Hadean			3,900 – 4,560			

人 类 起 源 时 间 表 The Evolutive Calendar

地球历史等于24小时 History of the earth = 24 hours		灵长类历史等于24小时 History of primates = 24 hours	
地球起源 Birth of the earth	午夜零点 Midnight	灵长类出现 Primates appears	10:15 am
生命起源 Birth of life	5:45 am	人类开始直立行走 First human ancestor walks upright	9:24 pm
脊椎动物起源 Birth of vertebrates	9:02 pm	直立人出现 *Homo erectus* appears	10:48 pm
哺乳动物起源 Birth of mammals	10.45 pm	现代人出现 Anatomically modern human appears	11:54 pm
灵长类的起源 Birth of primates	11.37 pm	发明文字 Invention of writing	11:59.45 pm
可能的人类起源 Possible birth of man	11.56 pm	建造金字塔 Pyramids built in Egypt	11:59.50 pm
南方古猿 Birth of *Australopithecus*	11.58 pm	哥伦布航海 Voyage of C. Columbus	1 second before midnight
智人起源 Birth of *Homo sapiens*	午夜前的6.5秒 6.5 seconds before midnight	计算机发明 Invention of PC	Now

资料来源：吴汝康《古人类学》，文物出版社，1989年；*Dragons of Eden*，by Carl Sagan．1977

Sources：Wu Rukang，*Paleoanthropology*，Cultural Relics Press，1989；Carl Sagan，*Dragons of Eden*，1977

长江中游文明之旅

后 记 Postscript

《郧县人——长江中游的远古人类》是湖北省博物馆举办的第一个旧石器文化的专题展览，本书是在同名展览的基础上编写的。

郧县人头骨化石是长江中游地区首次发现的最完整的人类头骨化石，它的发现填补了长江中游地区人类演化进程中的重要缺环，使该区域形成了从早更新世早期到晚更新世晚期较完整的古人类演化链，这在中国乃至世界都是罕见的。正因如此，我们以郧县人为重点，以湖北地区的古人类发现为线索，并辅以少量的世界其他地方的古人类演化材料，希望给一般读者简要介绍人类演化的历史。

该展览的筹备和本书的编写，我们得到了各文博、科研单位和个人的帮助和支持。谨向北京周口店遗址博物馆，中国科学院古脊椎动物与古人类研究所以及该所的高星、刘武、王雅志、张双北、郑绍华，中国自然博物馆高立红，湖北十偃市博物馆表示衷心的感谢。由于资料所限，湖北以外的旧石器遗存材料多为中国科学院古脊椎动物与古人类研究所提供。

湖北省文物考古研究所的李天元、冯小波在展览设想、展览体例和展览资料方面提供了详细的建议和无私的帮助，没有这样的帮助几乎就不可能完成本书的编写工作。该所的王善才、武仙竹也为本书的编写做了贡献。文物出版社第五图书编辑部为本书的出版付出了辛勤的劳动。中国对外翻译出版公司承担了本书的英文翻译，也特别向高宏、罗红燕、任京霞、陈兆娟、张晓璐和湖北省文化厅的宋乐静表示衷心的感谢。

最后，感谢湖北省财政厅为本书的出版提供了经费支持。

编 者
2007年8月

项目协调：张征雁

体例统筹：杨新改

整体设计：李　红

责任编辑：杨新改

设计制作：王慧英

责任印制：陆　联

图书在版编目（CIP）数据

　郧县人：长江中游的远古人类／湖北省博物馆　编.—

北京：文物出版社，2007.9

　（长江中游文明之旅）

　ISBN 978-7-5010-2249-6

　Ⅰ.郧… Ⅱ.湖… Ⅲ.文化遗址—考古发现—郧县

Ⅳ.K878.04

　中国版本图书馆CIP数据核字（2007）第094953号

郧县人——长江中游的远古人类

编　　者：湖北省博物馆

出版发行：文物出版社

地　　址：北京东直门内北小街2号楼

邮　　编：100007

网　　址：http://www.wenwu.com

邮　　箱：web@wenwu.com

经　　销：新华书店

制版印刷：北京雅昌彩色印刷有限公司

开　　本：889×1194毫米　　1/16

印　　张：6

版　　次：2007年9月第1版

印　　次：2007年9月第1次印刷

书　　号：ISBN 978-7-5010-2249-6

定　　价：98.00元